M000267227

The 9 Money Rules Millionaires Use: Only The Unconventional Ones

By Joel S. Salomon

ISBN: 0999280423
ISBN 13: 9780999280423

Contents

This book is dedicated to anyone who has ever been afraid of investing their money. You can do this! I believe in you!

Acknowledgements

Many, many people deserve and have my gratitude and appreciation for their help in making this book possible. The first, and subsequent, drafts were read by many friends and family members who offered emotional support and insightful thoughts as well. I wanted to highlight Rob Davidsen, Ada Lee, Seth Markowitz, Bruce Petersel, and Chara Rodriguera, for their awesome advice.

Similarly, Wayne Greenberg's patience with me during the recording of the audio book won't be soon forgotten.

Others who contributed in various ways include, but are not limited to, Ashley Adams, Diane Alter, Cheryl Amyx, Edwin Aristor, Andrea Beenham, Lake Begay, Peter Bemko, Leo Benavides, Craig Beresin, Mike Blanchard, Junau Boucard, Darnell Caballes, Dick Cagney, Mike Calandra, Jack Calcutt, Crystal Callahan, Danielle Capalino, Rita Lorraine Carey, Siyi Chen, Al Copersino, Katherine Copersino, Frank Coppola, Beth Davidsen, Julia De Sanctis, Thomas DeWolf, Andy Dooley, Mike Dooley, Liv Dzumaga, Santiago Echeverri, Andrew Edelsberg, Quentin English, Karen Feldman, John Felitto, Eddie Friedmann, Meris Gebhardt, Bob Glasspiegel, Mark Green, Howard Gursky, Holland Haiis, Rakale Hannah, Diana Hickert-Hill, Laura Hughes, Appio Hunter, Mark Hutchinson, Carl Hyppolite, Candice James, Engel Jones, Larry Kennedy, Kenneth Kim, Agam Kothari, Judith Lavendar, John Lee, Yossi Leon, Terri Liggins, Jukka Lipponen, Angie Maldonado, Anthony Marullo, Fran McCartan, Rob McInnes, Karl Mitchell, Beth Mohr, Kimi Nakamura, Jennifer Oh, Kim O'Neill, Laurie Ordile, Greig Paterson, Jim Patterson, Mike Perlin, John Phelan, Paul Pompeo, Riad Rehman, Jackie Roberge, Sean Ryan, Chris Salem, Ira Schnell, Julie Ann Segal, Maneesh Shanbhag, Illia Shapovalov, Tom Sheridan, Craig Slosberg, David Sochol, Martin Sterling, Anitha Suram, Katie Tarlin, Lindsey Tewell, Zach Thomas, Alexis Todd, David Tong, Mike Trager, Vicki Trager, Clarine Usher, Tony Vear, Marcos Velasquez,

Andy Vindigni, Emmett Walsh, John Watras, Bill Weidner, Mindi Wernick, Christy Whitman, Mike Zaremski, Mike Zarrilli, Karen Zhang.

In addition, I would be remiss if I didn't mention Terry Grundy's painstaking review of the manuscript. Thank you all for your support and help!

Foreword

I couldn't believe my eyes!

There's Joel, the nerdy financial hedge fund manager from New York climbing up a vine, yes, a vine hanging from a tree in the jungles of Peru, like Tarzan.

Instantly, in my view, Joel went from being a nerdy financial wizard to king of the jungle. And now you have the opportunity to read his incredibly insightful book: *The 9 Money Rules Millionaires Use.*

Every day you are faced with thousands of life changing decisions: which way you go will primarily come down to how much money you have.

Do you buy a new car or keep the one that's already paid for?

Do you send your kids to public school or private school?

Do you invest in the new tech start-up or go to Hawaii for fun?

Money is at the root of almost all your decisions. It's about time you learn the secrets of millionaires, so you can become one.

I remember meeting Joel in Santa Fe, New Mexico. We were both attending a conference called Infinite Possibilities Train the Trainer, which is awesome by the way. I was a guest speaker and Joel was in the audience. He immediately stood out to me because of his great smile and almost bald head. I notice bald guys in the audience because I too am bald and shiny.

At lunch, he introduced himself to me and I felt an instant connection. He told me he is on a mission to help over 100,000 people become financially free. Can you say awesome?!

Just ten months later Joel, Tarzan, was on stage speaking at the next Train the Trainer conference in New Orleans. WOW! Joel is a man of his word, as well as financial wisdom. And he takes inspired action! In New Orleans, he received a standing ovation. Son of a bitch. I spoke at the same event and did not get a standing ovation. This guy is dangerously awesome!

By buying his book, you made a brilliant decision to radically improve your financial situation and ideally become a millionaire and deepen your understanding of making money work for you, instead of you working for money.

Joel, a prosperity coach and former hedge fund manager, is an expert on investing and the law of attraction. His advice has dramatically improved my relationship with money. And opened my eyes to how easy it can be to manage and multiply my money. YAY!

As for me, I'm a SMART coach, author, artist, and expert on the Law of Attraction. I travel the world giving one-day workshops called Smart Manifesting. I've helped thousands of people manifest their dreams. But, one thing I see so many people struggling with is *money*. Even people who have a lot are worried. It's time to master your money and make money your friend.

Being the creative, artistic type of person I am, money has always been frustrating and confusing to me. I've made my share of financial investments over the years, some good, mostly bad.

I love Joel's book because he gives you simple DIY money managing tips that anyone can use. From tracking your monthly income and expenses, using credit to your advantage, to investing in real estate and why many mutual funds are not helpful for your financial freedom. I wish I would have read this book twenty years ago.

This book will show you how to cut through the financial jungle of confusion and multiply your money without working so darn hard, so you can do more of the things you love to do with those you love. Joel, Tarzan, to the rescue. But Joel, one word of advice, please don't shoot any more videos giving financial advice wearing a loincloth! Thank God YouTube took down that video. LOL.

Congratulations, you are now on your way to becoming a master of your money and mindset and joining the one hundred thousand-strong, financially free tribe of people who are putting money to work for them and living the life they want.

Abundantly yours,

Andy Dooley
Creator of Vibration Activation™
Andydooley.com

Introduction

"Hold out the possibility that what you have learned isn't true"

— Doug Nelson

"Her temperature is over 105!"

"Are you serious?"

"Yes! It's only gone up since you left and we gave her the children's Tylenol an hour ago and I started putting cold compresses on her. Anything else you want us to do?"

"No. We're going to come home!"

This was the conversation I had with my mom in early November of 2006. Morgan was not yet nine months old.

She had been waking up between 3:30 a.m. and 4:30 a.m. for months now.

I told Christine, my wife at the time, what was going on. We were on the Upper East Side of Manhattan with her sister for their birthdays (they are twins). I told Christine she should stay, but I really wanted to go home. Christine agreed to come with me, and we made the hour-long ride back home in a very unsettled state. We were both very worried, but obviously we couldn't do anything about it.

I know now that worrying is just "negative future planning." Since you can't do anything about the situation, why not think about what you do want to happen instead of what you don't?

But, at the time, we were both just anxious, upset and nervous. All feelings which can't serve you and will definitely cause more harm than good.

When we finally got home—I remember there being little traffic and we got home before 11:00 p.m.—we saw that Morgan was pale and clearly not herself.

We gave her more Tylenol at midnight and more cold washcloths. Her temperature eventually did go down below 104, but clearly it was still elevated and not normal.

We called her pediatrician and she told us to continue to do what we were doing, and if the temperature didn't go down on Sunday, to come in first thing Monday.

Morgan's temperature went down, but not much, and we decided to take her in to the pediatrician on Monday …

Why tell this story to start a book about money rules? Because this book is unconventional, as are the money rules you will be learning about herein! What you are going to learn is that one of the key rules is being grateful (Rule # 5) and it is essential to living the life of your dreams. Today, I am so grateful for Morgan being alive. But I am getting ahead of myself …

"Another book about money? Really?"

That is the feedback I received when I told my friends, family, former colleagues, and acquaintances I was writing another book.

"Why? Isn't this the most written-about subject?"

Well, yes, it is—perhaps besides Jesus!

But this book will teach you concepts about money that 'they' don't want you to know. I will teach you rules that should be broken. Rules that you were taught as 'truths.' I don't believe in truths! I only believe in empowering or limiting beliefs, and one empowering belief I have is there are no rules to become financially free except one: you must be financially literate. You must have a basic understanding of some terms and be able to use a calculator to divide, multiply, add, and subtract.

If you can do that, you are well on your way!

But what do you believe when it comes to money?

Do you believe that money is evil?

Do you believe that rich people are crooks and criminals?

Is it your belief that since your parents were poor, you must become poor?

Do you believe you have to work hard to become rich and successful?

I contend that all these are limiting beliefs which will stop you from becoming financially free. This is Rule #1—When You Believe! In Chapter 2, I will outline a specific technique that my clients use whenever they invest in any security to determine if they will make money.

Have you ever used your intuition, your sixth sense, to make a decision? Some will say, "I used my gut." Using your intuition—I call it your higher self—to invest is Rule #2. I actually play a game with my daughters whenever we are on vacation to help them develop their intuition, and I disclose it in Chapter 4.

Yes, I did say this book was unconventional, didn't I?

Another rule I will discuss is how your emotions can actually help you make money. Being happy is something rarely talked about by investment professionals. But I know from experience that when I was happy, I made more money (or lost less), and when I was really sad or depressed, I lost more (or made less). Check out Chapter 5 and you will learn that being happy (Rule #3) can help you become financially free.

Can you just sit at home all day and visualize your dreams and desires— your millions coming to you—and then they will appear? Of course not. You must take action! But when you are visualizing your dreams and desires, it will be inspired action! Visualizing is Rule #4, and in Chapter 6 you will get specific techniques on how to visualize, and then you will hear my experiences on manifesting dreams and desires.

You already heard about Rule #5. What are you grateful for? How does gratitude help you make money? You'll learn about the techniques I have incorporated into my life to use gratitude as a money-making tool.

Yes, when you give money away initially you have less money—in that moment in time. But within days or weeks or months you will have plenty of money to spare and share. Giving (Rule #6) does indeed change the world and it will change you and your relationship with money. Do you believe? Read chapter 8 for my experiences with giving and you will also read an award-winning speech I gave in 2018.

Do you budget (Rule #7)? Roll your eyes if you must, but you should know that at least 80 percent of millionaires know where their money is going, and where it is coming in from. I'm not saying you need to get out your Excel spreadsheet and do daily and monthly calculations every single month. What I *am* saying is that it would be helpful to consider where your money is going. I will discuss in detail why that will be helpful for you and your financial freedom in Part 2, Chapter 1. To me, financial freedom is the day your income from investments exceeds *all* your expenses—current or dream—so that you don't have to work if you don't want to.

This book will teach you that you can do it yourself (DIY—Rule #8). Another misconception that most everyone I meet—even professional investors—believe that you must turn your money over to the pros. We're taught that we are not smart enough, not good enough in math, or that we just don't have the time to do it. We are being shown this by all the financial institutions, large and small, *every day.*

We are taught that we must turn over our hard-earned (or not so hard-earned) money to our friendly financial advisor or planner (they used to be called stock brokers or insurance salesmen). She will then gladly charge us at least 1 percent—and sometimes much more—for this opportunity to help. Of course, this is on top of the fees you pay in commissions to buy or sell any stock, bond, mutual fund or ETF[1] (exchange-traded fund). Who will become financially free quicker—you or your financial adviser?

Do you diversify your investments? You do if you own even one mutual fund or put money into your retirement account[2] (also known as your Roth, SEP, 401[k], 403[b], or 457 plan). I will tell you why this may not be helpful in your quest to become financially free (Rule #9).

Why is this book different from every other money book you have read?

First of all, let me be clear. This book is not about 'getting rich quick!' Everyone is looking for the magic bullet, the amazing pill you can swallow and lose twenty-five lbs., the fountain of youth. I don't believe in any of that.

I do believe in financial discipline and education. I've been to many seminars presented by that "financial guru" teaching you how stock options, real estate, commodities or currencies (and today, cryptocurrencies) will be *the* way to make you rich. This book is not the one that will help you get rich tomorrow. I apologize for bursting your bubble.

I do, however, believe in getting rich! Some books will tell you "I am going to teach you how to get rich quick!" What does *quick* mean? Other books will say "Those books that teach you how to get rich quick are bogus! It can't be done!"

I give an example of a seminar that I went to, in Chapter 16 of my best seller, *Mindful Money Management: Memoirs of a Hedge Fund Manager,* that was touting how stock options will make you rich quick! And how that seminar changed my life.

Now, I believe that for some people—at least a few—that will actually happen. Quick might mean six months, twelve months or even two years. But if

---

1. An ETF is a marketable security that tracks an index of stocks, bonds, commodities or a basket of assets. The price of an ETF changes throughout the day as they are bought and sold unlike a mutual fund whose price only changes once a day.
2. See Part 2, Chapter 1 for a complete discussion on retirement plans including your 401k and Roth IRAs.

their financial freedom number is \$500,000 or \$1,000,000 they might actually achieve that. But—and this is a big but (not the posterior view, silly!)—more than 99 percent won't become financially free using stock options. And the reason is they won't get educated on the details of stock options (see my white paper on my website https://www.salaurmor.com/investing/) and they don't *believe* (see Chapter 2: "Rule #1: When You Believe").

What about getting rich slow? This is what most gurus teach and say you *must do*. So what does slow mean? I'd generally define it as "many years." It might be twenty to forty. Essentially, the "financial gurus" will tell you to save your money, watch compound interest work for you (see Chapter 1 for the "Rule of 72") and pay yourself first. Then when you're fifty-five if you're lucky—or sixty-five for some people, and much later for most—you will become financially free. That is "get rich slow!"

The processes in this book will take some time to implement and create financial freedom. But they do work. Be patient and know, when you implement change with grace and ease, it will develop. For some it will take months, for others it will take years. And, just like some of my clients, if you are not disciplined, you will never become financially free. I know that is harsh, but it is the truth.

It is difficult to challenge the status quo. In fact, most people won't do it for fear of getting ridiculed or having the haters come out of the shadows. It is not easy to stand up to a trillion-dollar industry and scream 'you are not right, reboot!'

But that is what this book is about. It is going to expose the flaws in the system—in the financial services industry.

The accepted truisms may not be true; they are just beliefs and limiting beliefs at that.

There are chinks in the armor. Be prepared for some soldiers to trip and fall.

And when there are chinks in the armor and you want protection, that protection can end up backfiring.

You don't actually have the protection you thought you had. In fact, you think you are safe, but then you trip and fall and get bitten by that rattlesnake in the grass.

Yes, sometimes the enemy is you yourself.

It may be self-sabotage; you are subconsciously stopping yourself from becoming financially free. Or you are so fearful of handling money, you give it to someone else, thinking you have released responsibility for it. And yet the person you release the responsibility to, causes you to lose money or maybe just not earn enough for you to ever become financially free.

Are you ready?

Are you open-minded?

Do you want to become consciously competent or, even better, unconsciously competent about making money?

Who should read this book? Are you teachable? Do you consider yourself "unconsciously incompetent?" That means you don't know what you don't know. Hopefully you are reading this book to become consciously competent. That is, to master self-awareness, be skilled in your investment decisions, and become financially literate.

What would be even better would be to become unconsciously competent. An example of this is when you learn to drive. The first few times you drive to the train station, you have to think about all the turns. You have to be conscious about putting your blinkers on to make the turn. And then you have to think about actually turning the steering wheel. Also, putting your foot on the brake or the accelerator. But after some time—for me over thirty years now—I am completely unconsciously competent in driving to the train station. Some mornings, I have no idea how I got there. I don't remember one turn I have made, because I was thinking about a client becoming financially free.

Becoming unconsciously competent in investing and investment decision-making means you don't even have to think about whether the action you are taking is correct or not; you just *know* it's the right decision. You know you will be making money.

This book is split up into two parts. The first part is where you get to be inspired. You will learn how important it is to feel gratitude, happiness, and connect with your higher self, by trusting your intuition. You will learn that you have to believe, have faith, and know that being abundant is your birthright. Then, in the second part of the book, we will go through the processes to take some inspired action toward financial freedom.

Just *know* that you will move in that direction in this book. Let's begin!

PART
1

Are you Open-Minded?

1

Unconventional Rules

"That can't be done. No one is going to hire you if you don't have an MBA."

"What?"

"There is no way a hedge fund or mutual fund will hire you unless you get 'sell-side' equity analyst experience."

These were the conversations (actually one side of the conversations) I was having with actuaries on Wall Street in the early 1990s. You had to follow the path of going to a rating agency, getting the absolutely necessary experience there as a credit analyst. Then you had to go to a Wall Street bank or investment bank like J.P. Morgan Chase, Goldman Sachs, Morgan Stanley, Citigroup, or any of a dozen foreign banks. While there, you had to work for a senior equity analyst covering the industry you wanted to invest in, and then—and only then—could you make the leap to an analyst on the buy side. And only after you had sufficient experience as an analyst at one of these "bulge-bracket" firms could you make the move to be a portfolio manager actually managing money. Well, I didn't follow that path.

I'm an anti-rules guy. If you tell me this is how something *has* to be done, I will find another way to do it. This happened when my father told me early on in high school that "We can't afford to send you to a private university, so you should think about the New York state schools like Binghamton or Albany or Stony Brook." These were all good-to-great schools at the time, but I don't like to follow the rules. I'm a contrarian at heart.

So, I asked my dad: "What would it take for me to go to a private school? How much would I have to save?" And what if I found a private university that charged an amount that was close to a state school? What if I paid for one year and then took out loans for the rest? He laughed and said "If you can save at least one full year of tuition, you can go to a private school!"

I had no idea what I was getting myself into, but besides being a contrarian and anti-rules kind of guy, I was also very competitive and goal oriented. Give me a challenge and I will find a way to achieve my goal.

So, I started working—hard! First, it was being a little league umpire; then it was Nathans. I kept on asking my boss there if I could work more hours. But there were limits that a kid in the tenth grade with school from 8:00 a.m. to almost 3:00 p.m. could work, especially if he wanted to do his homework and get good grades. But the summers were different. I could work more! And then there was grade twelve, when I could work even more, because my coursework in the second half of the year was pretty easy.

Yes, I achieved the goal, but I continued to work hard after I entered the University of Rochester. I remember the summer after freshman year. I had my job at Nathans that I worked at from 4:00 p.m. to 9:00 p.m. most evenings, but what about during the day? I applied to work at some local places and actually got a job at Burger & Shake, a local hamburger joint in Farmingdale, New York that was looking for a busboy for the early morning shift and lunch crowd as well.

I had the honor of sweeping floors, cleaning toilets, and even filling potholes in the parking lot when the morning rush had eased and the lunch crowd had not yet started. That summer, I also had the privilege of selling Cutco knives—mostly to friends of my parents and grandparents. I still remember the advertisement my mother found in the Long Island newspaper, *Newsday*, that read:

✳✳✳ Make $1,000 Easily ✳✳✳

Wow, that was 10 percent of the annual tuition. Along with my other jobs, I could pay 30–40 percent of the full, one-year tuition.

What did I have to do? Give 'only' one hundred presentations to potential customers and they would pay ten dollars per presentation. I didn't have to sell anything! So, I went and got 'trained.' And then I started giving presentations to all my parents' friends—luckily, a large group! And I got to thirty presentations really quickly.

I think I sold one or two knife sets, but honestly, who cared? The goal was to get to one hundred presentations. But that is not what the district sales representative wanted. We had to turn in our statistics weekly. After four weeks of just two sales total and over forty presentations, he insisted on joining me on my next presentation. I was quite resistant. Was this really part of the requirement to get to one hundred?

Well, the next presentation I had was a good friend of my mom's. So, that next night, I ventured out to Massapequa Park in my mom's car to sell a set of steak knives. I did the whole routine: showing how the scissors could cut through rope and the best knife could cut a frozen bagel! After all this razzle-dazzle, I asked for the sale. And Winny proclaimed that she was a vegetarian and really didn't need steak knives. I thanked her for her time and got signature number forty-two (just fifty-eight more to go!).

After we left, the sales director harangued me: "How could you not prequalify this lead? Didn't you know she wasn't a steak eater?" After five minutes of this, he decided we should go back in and sell her the vegetable chopper. *Really? Do we have to? I already have my signature*, I thought …

But no; he walked me back in and presented the chopper himself. She looked at me angrily when she saw us back at her front door, but thankfully, he was quick. And she graciously said 'no thanks.' And we were on our way.

Fortunately, he didn't come out with me again since he felt I had learned my lesson. I soon started running out of my parents' friends and went to my grandparents' friends. I reached over fifty sales presentations before I realized summertime was running thin (just three weeks to go). And I was also running dry on relatives and friends. I had forgotten one of the key items of sales: ask for referrals at the end of every presentation, whether they buy or not).

Well, I did learn a lot about selling when I was nineteen. The most important lesson was dealing with rejection. I definitely received at least fifty "No's." I did manage to get into the high single digits in sales, but I never did reach the hundred presentations. I guess it sounded much easier than it was.

However, I did manage to earn over two thousand dollars that summer, and that, along with all my other odd jobs over the last four years, was enough to pay for more than one full year of tuition.

Maybe the most important experience I gained from selling Cutco knives was meeting Karen, my first girlfriend. She was the daughter of one of my parents' friends. They also happened to be one of the few sales I made that summer—coincidence? I don't believe in coincidences! She also became my first love and we dated for almost two years. Karen and I reconnected in 2016. See Chapter 6 for how and why I truly believe in synchronicities, not coincidences!

What path *did* I follow to become a portfolio manager? Well, for those who haven't read the best seller, *Mindful Money Management: Memoirs of a Hedge Fund Manager*, I highly recommend you buy a copy https://www.salaurmor.com/salaurmor-shop/ and take a look at Chapter 2: "My Dream Job—Or Is it?" But here is a very quick synopsis of my path:

I became a Fellow of the Society of Actuaries (FSA) in May 1992 while I was working at New York Life Insurance Company. Though I was having some fun working there, I had a lot more fun in the evenings and weekends when I was analyzing stocks. My key question to myself back then was, *how do I align my hobby and my career?*

Yes, I did call up lots of actuaries on Wall Street and got those answers. Finally, I found an actuary who told me his 'secret.' He advised me to start working at a rating agency. If you want to move to the buy side—that is, invest in the stocks or bonds of insurers—the best place to learn is a rating agency.

Both Moody's Investors Service and Standard and Poor's Rating Service were touted as great training grounds. They said that I would be able to utilize my actuarial skills to analyze financial statements, get access to insurers' cash flow testing and reserve adequacy analysis, and be able to determine the creditworthiness of those insurers. Not only that, they said—but I would have the opportunity to upgrade or downgrade companies, assign ratings to debt securities, write up special reports on important industry issues, and create research reports on individual companies.

Additionally, I would be able to travel!

The analysis aspects sounded awesome. The job description also appealed to my second-biggest passion after investing, which is traveling. I was hooked.

So, I started working at Moody's Investors Service in 1993.

The next step those actuaries on Wall Street prescribed was to get a job at one of the big banks. Did I do that?

No!

Here is where my route to becoming a hedge fund manager was truly unconventional. I didn't follow the traditional path—the *rule*. Everyone said you had to get a job as an associate at one of those big banks: Citi, J.P. Morgan Chase, Bank of America, Merrill Lynch, Goldman Sachs, or Morgan Stanley. Then work your way up to a senior analyst covering insurance companies, then—and only then—could you possibly get a job at a hedge fund or mutual fund. And that job would be a senior analyst, not a portfolio manager. But if you did well picking stocks at that fund, eventually they would promote you to a fund manager. Or you could leave the firm and get a job at another fund as a portfolio manager.

Well, my next job was at Swiss Reinsurance Company.

Why?

A recruiter called me and said that a reinsurer was making private equity (PE) investments and was looking for an analyst. I jumped at the chance to interview and quickly realized during the process that the job was much more than a PE analyst.

This group at Swiss Re was on the cutting edge of financial markets. They were structuring credit enhancements (a method whereby a company attempts to improve its creditworthiness) for individual insurance blocks of business and trying to do the same for whole companies. And they were managing the existing PE portfolio.

Now, I realized this wasn't public securities (the kind traded on exchanges, with constantly updated prices like you see crawling across the bottom of the TV screen on CNBC). But I also realized that it was getting me one step closer to my dream job. So, I took it!

But who knew that I really took this job so that I could get laid off, move to Zurich, and travel all over Europe for almost a year and a half?

When I got back to New York in 2000, I realized that I really wasn't one step closer to my dream job and eventually started looking for it. But I did have doubts (now I tell my clients to "Doubt the Doubt!") and I actually found an opportunity at a small hedge fund that was looking for an equity and credit analyst. After three short years, I received a call from my Citi equity salesperson asking me if I was interested in being a portfolio manager there. My dream job—well, almost. I say "almost," because my dream was really to have my own company.

I started at Citi in January, 2008. Yes, it took me fifteen years, but I did succeed in my dream of managing money. And as all of you know who read *Mindful Money Management*, I did eventually start my own hedge fund in 2013.

No, I didn't follow the 'rule' of going to the sell-side[1] to become a money manager. I did make the leap from credit rating agency to industry to analyst to money manager though. And, no, I don't have an MBA.

I get asked all the time: "how can you become a money manager without an MBA?" or, "how can you become a money manager without working on the sell-side?" In fact, one client of mine asked me to teach him how to transition from having a job as an actuary to a career as a money manager.

My answer is in the next chapter when we discuss beliefs. Having faith or absolute belief (Rule #1) or a 'knowing,' means believing in your dreams. Because as Napoleon Hill said in one of my favorite books, the *New York Times* best seller *Think and Grow Rich*: "Whatever the mind of man can conceive, and bring himself to believe, he can achieve." For a list of my favorite books, please see here: https://www.salaurmor.com/inspiration/#books.

Let me give you one final example of not following the rules. When I was twelve years old, I went to the orthodontist with my parents. My dentist had suggested I go because of my "buck" teeth; both my front teeth were jutting out of my mouth at an angle.

Well, we went. And, after the exam, the orthodontist explained to me and my parents that to actually be able to wear braces, I had to get four teeth pulled! There simply wasn't enough space for my front teeth to move back. And without the teeth being removed, there was nowhere for them to go.

So with this newly alarming knowledge, I just had to ask, "Isn't there any other way? Four teeth is a lot of teeth to get pulled out, isn't it?!"

---

1. A "sell-side firm" is a general term for a company that sells investment services to asset management firms.

And of course, I was fearful. I was worried and scared about the pain I would have to endure, even though the orthodontist assured me they would give my local anesthesia so that I wouldn't feel a thing.

"Well, there is one other way, but it is a real long shot," the orthodontist explained.

"Okay. I am listening," I responded.

"I can have you fitted for a night brace. If you wear it as much as possible—even during the day most days—then there is a chance that the night brace could move the teeth enough that you wouldn't have to have them pulled."

"Done!" I said without thinking about the ramifications of having a wire coming out of my mouth and wrapping around my neck all day long in junior high school (teenagers can be mean, but that is another story).

So, I got fitted for this contraption. And I did what wasn't "supposed to be done." I wore that night brace every waking and sleeping moment except when I was eating: 22 hours and sometimes 23 hours; I ate my meals real fast in those days!

Three months later, I went back to that orthodontist. And he had good news. "If you continue to do what you are doing for the next six weeks, you won't have to have *any* teeth pulled."

Well, I was determined to break my own record of 155.75 hours of wearing that night brace. And I did! Two of those six weeks, I broke 161 hours (for those interested, that meant more than 23 hours on average per day for the week). And thankfully, I did not have even one tooth pulled.

So ... *what* rules? Tell me what can't be done and I will find a way around it.

As Napoleon Hill said in the classic *Think and Grow Rich*, "Nothing is impossible to the person who backs desire with enduring faith." And he continued: "A great many years ago I purchased a fine dictionary. The first thing

I did with it was to turn to the word 'impossible,' and neatly clip it out of the book. That would not be an unwise thing for you to do."

Though I didn't read this book until 2008, I feel like some of the key lessons I read then were in my being thirty years earlier!

The title of this chapter is "Unconventional Rules." So, let's discuss what each word means.

What does "unconventional" mean?

According to the Merriam-Webster Dictionary, it means not conventional. It means not bound or in accordance with convention; being out of the ordinary.

Are you ordinary?

Do you want to be ordinary? I certainly don't!

"Special"—wouldn't that be great if you were special. Or "unusual."

We all have our own concept of money. Is it currency? A measure of exchange of value? What does money mean to you? To me, money is the assets or property or financial resources that you own. Money is wealth. But you can also be wealthy in terms of abundance and prosperity. Money is just one way to be wealthy (see Part 2, Chapter 2 for a much fuller explanation on money and what it means to me).

Now, let's talk about rules.

Again, according to the Merriam-Webster Dictionary, a rule is a prescribed guide for conduct or action; a law or regulation prescribed by the founder of a religious order for observance by its members; an accepted procedure, custom, or habit.

The second-level definition is: a usually valid generalization; a generally prevailing quality, state or mode; or a determinate method for performing a mathematical operation and obtaining a certain result.

The third-level definition is: an exercise of authority or control; a period during which a specified ruler or government exercises control.

I particularly like the second-level definition involving mathematical operations. Maybe that is self-evident for readers who know I graduated from the University of Rochester with a double major in both mathematics and statistics.

Most important of all is number three though. I really dislike being controlled. However, one of my many teachers in this lifetime taught me a great lesson that I try to live by: "To get control, you must give up control."

It may sound somewhat devious, but I will tell you I have been giving up control ever since. And the few times I have tried to be controlling since then, it backfired. When you are controlling and the person you are trying to control is as well, it invariably leads to arguments and maybe even worse!

In the foreword to the best seller, *12 Rules for Life* by Professor Jordan Peterson, Dr. Norman Dodge explains Peterson's rules: "He tells stories to bring to bear his knowledge of many fields as he illustrates and explains why the best rules do not ultimately restrict us, but instead facilitate our goals and make for fuller, freer lives … and that is because alongside our wish to be free of rules, we all search for structure."

Dr. Dodge's explanation is why I enjoyed Peterson's book so much. Yes, the best rules are not restrictive; they just help us achieve our goals. That is the point of this book. To help you achieve your goals. And what are those goals for you? I recommend you pause for a moment here and write down your goals when it comes to money and financial freedom. Don't put a time frame on them though (see Part 2, Chapter 3 for why).

Finally, Abraham Hicks, in one of the many seminars held around the globe, had this to say about rules:

"… It's like working somewhere where there are lots of rules, and so those rules … inspire your action. 'Oh, I can't do that. Oh, I can't do that.' Well, that's a hard way to live, rather than being free to follow your inspiration. It's … having to stop at a stoplight in the middle of the night when there's no traffic coming from any direction and sit there for the full two minutes and 30 seconds until that light decides to free you from your bondage. And every fiber of your being says, 'this just doesn't make any sense. But if I break this rule, there's probably a policeman in the bushes who's trolling for revenue who will give me grief.'

"And so you … trained yourself to do illogical things because other people have rules and requirements. And … a lot of your behavior … is offered because you're worried about the negative thing that will happen if you don't do it rather than because you're inspired by your inner being's understanding of what lovely road this will take you down."

Before I end this chapter on rules, I want to discuss an easy rule to remember to use when investing. It is called the "Rule of 72." Of course, it's not really a rule. It is just an easy way to compute compound interest quickly.

And it can be used to see how quickly your money will double. For example, if you know that an investment will return 8 percent a year on average, then your money will double in nine years (72/8—just take off the percentage). If you know that an investment will return 24 percent, then your money will double in just three years (72/24). This is a great rule to easily calculate how much money you will have after a certain time period (and a great pub game too!).

Suppose you want to know how much money you will have in eighteen years and you are investing in an asset that will return 8 percent. Well, we just found out it will double in nine years. So, in eighteen years, the asset will double again or go up by four times in total. If you started with $1,000, you will have four times that or $4,000 at the end of eighteen years.

Similarly, if your return is 24 percent annually and someone asked you how much money will you have in nine years, you know that since it doubles in three years, doubles again in another three, and doubles again in another three, that in nine years you will have eight times (2x2x2) your money. So, if you again start with $1,000, in just nine years, your investment will have grown to $8,000.

This is the power of compound interest.

In Jeff Olsen's groundbreaking book, *The Slight Edge*, he tells the story of the King who gives his two sons a choice. They can have $1 million the next day, or they can have a penny which will double every day for thirty days. They both get to decide in the morning. The first son stays up all night calculating, while the second son makes his choice immediately.

Who wouldn't want $1,000,000 to invest? The second son goes out and hires his investment counselors and they make their allocations to various types of assets, from gold bullion to currencies and various securities.

The first son chooses the penny and waits and waits and waits. Meanwhile, the second son is making some gains—and some losses—but his money is compounding. By the end of the period, he has been able to earn almost 5 percent on his money. That is a pretty impressive amount for just 30 days. However, after paying his advisors their fees, his $1,000,000 is actually down slightly.

The first son's money has accumulated to more than $2.1 million! He didn't pay any advisors or planners. He was able to have more than double the money that his brother got. And all because of the power of compound interest.

Jeff tells the story to emphasize the importance of time and how doing little things every day can really pay off hugely over long periods of time. It is important to note that he is not saying that your money will double every day nor every year for thirty years. In fact, a really good return on investment would be if your money doubled every nine years (the return on investment is 8 percent).

As Professor Jordan Peterson states in *12 Rules For Life*, "… don't underestimate the power of vision and direction. These are irresistible forces able to transform what might appear to be unconquerable obstacles into trends, reversible pathways, and expanding opportunities. Strengthen the individual. Start with yourself. Take care of yourself. Define who you are, refine your personality, choose your destination, and articulate your being. As Nietzsche so brilliantly, noted: 'He whose life has a why can bear almost any how.'"

So, what's your goal, your vision, your direction? What is your "why?" If you don't know, that is okay; hopefully, many of these answers will come to you over the coming chapters. I believe in you!

Key Points from Chapter 1:

- Go to your dictionary and cut out the word 'impossible.'

- Some (most?) rules are meant to be broken.

- Write down all the possibilities to achieve your goals. Don't stop writing until you have at least five, and don't second-guess yourself.

- If 'conventional' wisdom says you must take specific steps to achieve your goals, ask why! Know that there is no one right answer to achieving your dreams and desires.

- As Napoleon Hill said in his *New York Times* best seller, *Think and Grow Rich*, "Nothing is Impossible to the person who backs desire with enduring faith."

- Don't assume all rules are a given and must be true. Challenge conventional wisdom and do what feels right (see Chapter 4 for more on how to tap into your feelings and intuition).

- Play the game "Rule of 72" with friends to see how quickly your favorite investment will increase in value.

Rule #1: When You Believe

"There can be miracles when you believe. Though hope is frail, it's hard to kill. Who knows what miracles you can achieve when you believe. Somehow you will. You will when you believe."

— Whitney Houston and Mariah Carey, Lyrics from "When You Believe."

This song is definitely one of my favorites and one I listen to every day as part of my morning routine. You can find the full lyrics to this powerful song here: https://www.salaurmor.com/inspiration/#lyrics

"It is your actions that most accurately reflect your deepest beliefs—those that are implicit, embedded into your being, underneath your conscious apprehensions ... You can only find out what you actually believe (rather than what you think you believe) by watching how you act. It takes careful observation, and education, and reflection, and communication with others, just to scratch the surface of your beliefs." — Jordan Peterson from *12 Rules For Life*

Jordan goes on to describe the Dragon Story by Jack Kent. He explains that it is a very simple story: "It's about a small boy, Billy Bixby, who spies a dragon sitting on his bed one morning. It's about the size of a house cat and he tells his mother about it, but she tells him there's no such thing as a dragon. So, it starts to grow. It eats all of Billy's pancakes. Soon, it fills the whole house. Mom tries to vacuum, but she must go in and out of the house, and through the windows because the dragon is everywhere. It takes forever. Then, the dragon runs off with the house. Billy's dad comes home and there's just an empty space where they used to live. The mailman tells him where the house went. He chases after it, climbs up the dragon's head and neck and rejoins his wife and son. Mom still insists the dragon does not exist, but Billy, who's pretty much had it by now insists: 'There is a dragon, Mom.' Instantly, it starts to shrink. Soon, it's cat-sized again. Everyone agrees that dragons of that size (1) exist and (2) are much preferable to their gigantic counterparts. Mom, eyes reluctantly opened by this point, asks why it had to get so big. Billy quietly suggests: 'maybe it wanted to be noticed.'"

Well, maybe *not* maybe.

What is your interpretation of that story? Mine is that beliefs can be really powerful. As can those who want to be noticed!

In John Felitto's powerful book, *The 90-Day Game*, he discusses the five key ingredients that set a "fertile environment for belief formation." He describes the five factors as:

1. Suggestibility

2. Authority figures

3. Emotional resonance

4. Interpretations

5. Reinforcement

By this he means that beliefs (Rule # 1) are developed because we take suggestions (#1) from others easily, especially if they are from people like our parents, teachers, bosses, peer group, and others we look up to (#2). Beliefs are also established when our feelings like happiness, fear, sadness, guilt, etc. are attached to them. Think of when we are young children and a parent who you rely on for food, clothing, and shelter is angry or mad at you (#3). Finally, two people may interpret the same event differently (#4), and if the same event happens many times, we will interpret them the same way (#5).

Here is an example from my own life: When I was twelve years old, I was on stage at Unqua Elementary School in Massapequa, Long Island. It was my sixth-grade play, and when it came time to say my lines, I just froze for what seemed like thirty minutes—to me. Finally, they skipped over me and no one remembered those ten or twenty seconds except for me—for the next forty years! In fact, if you asked me to speak in front of more than two people, I would bring my note cards or a paper to read off of.

I remember after the play my parents asking me what happened, and I felt embarrassed and sad. Here is where numbers one, two, and three came in. The interpretation came from me. I had already been feeling embarrassed or out of place whenever I was put "on the spot" during school. I was almost always prepared, but when I wasn't—especially in French class—I felt ridiculed by other kids (I distinctly remember being called "Guy Le Snob."). My interpretation of the sixth-grade play incident and the many monologues in middle and high school was that "I am not good enough."

This was reinforced for many, many years. I remember giving a speech at New York Life Insurance Company in front of the other actuarial associates. I prepared for weeks in advance and read my notes!

I also distinctly remember when my manager at Swiss Re in Zurich asked me to speak in front of all of the executives of the Swiss Re New Markets Division. There must have been almost four hundred people in the auditorium at the conference in Schruns, Austria.

Charlotte asked me to speak as a "reward" for doing a good job while I worked for her from January 1999 to January 2000. To me, obviously, that was more like a severe punishment.

"What did I do to deserve this?!" I kept on asking myself. But I made sure I was prepared: I wrote up my PowerPoint slides and put notes together for every single page—even the graphs and charts. And when it came time to do my speech, I walked up to the podium with fifty index cards and I read each and every note.

I do remember about fifteen minutes into my speech getting the courage to look up. And in the second row, there was the President of the division and his right-hand man both with their heads down, sleeping!

Well, I put my head right back into my notes and read the last ten minutes of that speech. That was reinforcement (#5). So, even as recently as 2015 and 2016, when I was a hedge fund manager, I continued to tell myself the same story: "You are a terrible public speaker. You are not good enough. No one wants to hear what you have to say."

In fact, I went to lunches and dinners in which various money managers and analysts would "pitch" their best stock ideas. They would all ramble on for five to ten minutes without any notes. I came prepared with at least two pages written up and I read my prearranged remarks. I didn't look up, for fear of someone's head being in their ice cream or chocolate cake.

To be open with you, I've come a long way in the last few years. You'll definitely want to read my story in Chapter 8 about giving a speech at Mike Dooley's Infinite Possibilities Train the Trainer Course in New Orleans in March of 2018. In fact, in just two years, I've presented more than sixty times to groups ranging from five to two hundred and fifty.

"Being Defeated is often a Temporary Condition. Giving up is what makes it Permanent."

— Marilyn vos Savant

In his groundbreaking, *New York Times* best-selling book, *Sapiens*, Yuval Noah Harari delves into the difference between "objective," "subjective," and "inter-subjective." For our purposes here, it is interesting to focus on how these views impact our beliefs. Yuval states that an objective phenomenon exists "independently of human consciousness and human beliefs." He gives the example of radioactivity not being a "myth." It doesn't matter if you believe or disbelieve radioactivity; if you are exposed long enough to materials that are radioactive, you will likely die of a disease caused by overexposure to radioactive materials.

Yuval describes the subjective as "something that exists depending on the consciousness and beliefs of a single individual." He gives the example of a child who believes in the existence of an imaginary friend who only exists in the child's "subjective consciousness" and when the child grows out of it (i.e., stops believing that the friend exists), then the imagined "fades away."

Most important for my upcoming discussion on Diversification (Part 2, Chapter 5) is "inter-subjective," which he says is "something that exists within the communication network linking the subjective consciousness of many individuals." Yuval goes on to explain that "the dollar, human rights, the United States of America all exist in the shared imagination of billions." He states that imagined orders are inter-subjective, which implies that to change them, you must simultaneously change the consciousness of billions of people. This obviously is not easy.

What are your beliefs (Rule #1) when it comes to money?

Do you believe you are born to achieve massive wealth?

Do you believe you are worthy?

As a prosperity coach, I tell my clients to write down their belief level for each investment idea they have where "1" is massive doubt: *That's really, really risky! Can't I lose all my money in that investment?* And "10" is absolute faith: *I know that I am going to make tons of money in this investment.*

Let me give you an example (Let me be clear that I am not recommending you buy cryptocurrencies; it is only an example): On November 24th, 2017, two guys buy bitcoin at $8,000. One guy has been researching it all year and decided it was an awesome investment opportunity. He's a "10." The second guy had gotten a tip from a friend that it was going higher. He buys one bitcoin, though he has massive doubt; he is a "1." Less than a week later, bitcoin is worth about $10,000. The first guy is so happy. "I told you, it was going higher," he says. The second guy worries, "I hope it doesn't go back down."

A few days later bitcoin is back at $8,800. The first guy doubles down and buys more. "This is the best buying opportunity out there," he explains.

The second guys sells! He is really worried and believes this is risky and complete speculation. He is so happy he made a little bit of money on bitcoin.

Less than three weeks later, bitcoin hits its all-time high of $19,500. The guy who *knew* he was going to make money sells. He makes almost 250 percent in less than one month. The second guy has no idea where bitcoin is trading. He is worried about losing money elsewhere.

In *Flourish*, a book by best-selling author, Martin Seligman, beliefs are alluded to throughout. Martin states in relation to the stock market that, "Optimism causes the market to go up and pessimism causes it to go down." He then goes on to state that, "... stocks go up when people are optimistic about their future worth and they go down when people are pessimistic about their future worth. There is no real value, of the stock or a derivative, that can be independent of the perceptions and expectations of investors' perceptions about what price that piece of paper will have in the future."

However, he also goes on to talk about fundamentals (See Part 2, Chapter 4) of stocks: "I hasten to add that optimism and pessimism are not the whole story ... some investors are still concerned with fundamentals. In the long run, fundamentals anchor ... the price of the stock, with the price fluctuating broadly around the value of the fundamentals, but with the short-run price heavily influenced by optimism and pessimism ... the value of fundamentals is influenced, even if it is not determined, by the market's expectation of the future value of the fundamentals."

What is your belief level that you are going to make or lose money in each investment idea you own or are thinking about owning?

Write it down, assuming you haven't done this when you bought the investment.

And if it isn't at least an 8 or 9 or 10, sell it, or don't get involved!

Until you get your belief level high enough, it is very likely that you are going to be selling when you should be buying. Your doubt and fear will lead to inappropriate investment decisions just like the second guy in the example above.

Do you have absolute faith in your investments, or massive doubt? Or are you somewhere in between, but closer to massive doubt?

In T. Harv Eker's #1 *New York Times* best seller, *Secrets of The Millionaire Mind,*™ he sets forth powerful statements regarding the beliefs of the poor compared to the rich.

First, Eker recommends that "If you want to get rich, you will have to change your inner blueprint to fully believe you are every bit as good as any millionaire or multimillionaire out there."

Here are just a few of them to consider:

1. "You can be a kind, loving, caring, generous, and spiritual person and be really frickin' rich."

2. "Rich people act in spite of fear. Poor people let fear stop them."

3. "There's nothing wrong with getting a steady paycheck, unless it interferes with your ability to earn what you're worth. There's the rub. It usually does."

4. "Rich people believe 'I create my life.' Poor people believe 'life happens to me.'"

5. "Rich people play the money game to win. Poor people play the money game to *not* lose."

As a Certified Infinite Possibilities Trainer and Trailblazer (I trained more than six people for at least six hours about Mike Dooley's *New York Times* best seller, *Infinite Possibilities*), I would be remiss if I didn't discuss Mike

Dooley's powerful book and his views on beliefs—which I wholeheartedly agree with.

First, he makes it clear that our beliefs come first. They influence our thoughts, words, and actions, and the whole world around us. And as you believe, so you think.

So, how do you change your life? Change your beliefs!

Well, how do you do that? Nothing is easy unless you believe it is easy. To change your thoughts and your life and destiny, you must first master your beliefs.

Are your beliefs limiting or empowering?

Do you believe that diversification makes you more money?

Do you believe diversification stops you from losing money?

We will talk more about diversification in Part 2, Chapter 5. But let me just introduce the concept that what you believe may not be serving you and may be a "limiting belief." If you believed people are generally dishonest and that something bad is going to happen, then when your house is robbed, what was the cause and what was the effect? Did your belief create the thought which created the life experience, or did the life experience produce the belief which created the thought?

My belief is: "It doesn't really matter!" Your house was robbed and wouldn't it be great if you could install some new "empowering beliefs" (as Dooley calls them) to ensure this doesn't happen again? Well, he recommends one way to install new beliefs is to begin by creating change first with your thoughts, words, and actions. By changing what you think and do, you'll gradually begin changing your life experiences which will gradually change your beliefs.

His three-step process for installing new beliefs is first to choose beliefs that serve your life. For example, some empowering beliefs around money might be to believe that "I am wealthy, abundant, and deserving. And I am worthy of all the wealth that I seek."

The second step is to choose these beliefs through your thoughts and words. "Money is everywhere and comes easily to me."

And the third step is to "act as if" these beliefs are already true every day. How do you do that? By behaving in ways that reinforce them. When you get out of bed, make your breakfast, and decide how you will get to work. Maybe splurge once a month by taking a limousine. I'm not recommending going into debt to do this though!

What limiting beliefs do you have?

Let me tell you that how changing my beliefs helped me. One of my biggest limiting beliefs was: "you have to work hard to be rich and successful."

Was anyone taught this growing up? I was by my parents and I am pretty sure their parents taught them this, my great-grandparents taught my grandparents, and so on. But I will tell you this is just a limiting belief.

I started working for Citigroup in January 2008. This was my first job right after I got divorced at the end of 2007, in which I would get paid for performance. I figured I would just work super hard and I would become rich and successful. Well, some of you may remember that 2008 was not the best year in the stock market; the most popular index dropped 40 percent.

I got to work at 7:15 a.m., worked most nights to 9:00 p.m., and got home after 10:30 p.m. Then I got up at 5:30 a.m. or so and did it all over again. I did earn a tiny bonus that year, but I was burning myself out. And I realized that if I kept up that pace, I wouldn't be around to enjoy any riches if they indeed did ever come. See, I wasn't exercising. I was eating calorie-rich food, drinking lots of coffee and caffeinated sodas (with that poisonous, high-fructose corn syrup), and gaining lots of weight.

In 2009, I decided to change my beliefs, words, thoughts, and actions. I started spending my evenings and weekends when I didn't have my daughters, socializing. I was present with my daughters, not analyzing a company or checking emails constantly like I did in 2008. I wasn't working seventy-five to eighty hours a week. I was having more balance in my life and enjoying my work more. I was happy, and a funny thing happened. I was more productive. I even started saying to myself I can work smarter and be rich and successful. And I was.

And as I discussed in *Mindful Money Management*, 2009 was the year I earned multiples of what I had ever earned in my life. This is proof that changing my beliefs worked.

In 2012, I decided to pursue my dream: starting a hedge fund. I actually received oral commitments from two companies to give me money to manage, but, in December 2012, both companies dropped out. I had already moved into commercial real estate space in Manhattan, committed to paying a lawyer, accountant, auditor, prime broker, fund administrator, and a company that had a database that I could use to analyze insurers—all without any money. Money was flowing, just not *in*.

I could have given up. But I *acted as if* we had the money already. I did some "crazy" things. I hired an analyst in January of 2013. I started interviewing Chief Financial Officers. And my analyst and I put together a mock portfolio in a spreadsheet and checked our 'performance' every day. We had morning meetings to discuss our best ideas and make changes to the portfolio. We even called companies that we were "invested" in.

And, of course, I spent a lot of time pounding the phones and calling everyone I knew, begging for money. We had a great meeting with an investor on January 25th, and at the end of February—less than two months later—we received a commitment letter saying they were going to invest. I truly believe by *acting as if* we already had the money, we received the money!

Let me give another example that Mike Dooley highlights in his best seller, *Infinite Possibilities*. First, he makes it clear that "our actions are our *beliefs in motion*." That is, how we act links the present we know about to the future that we expect. He states that if you believe that your fellow "adventurers are kind and wonderful, you greet them with open arms." And of course, if you believe that you are the creator of your own reality, then you accept complete "responsibility for all that has ever happened in your life, while behaving responsibly." Thus, it implies that we "automatically act in line with our beliefs."

He goes on to say that if you knew without a doubt—with absolute certainty—that all you had to do to write an "internationally best-selling novel was to put pen to paper … would you do it?" Of course you would!

Another example of *acting as if* is when you get an unexpectedly large bill. Instead of complaining, you can do what Mike Dooley does and say "It's a good thing I'm rich." Now, even if you aren't—yet—once you start doing it, you start believing it and feeling it.

Consider what things you are doing that implicitly are having you *act as if* you need more money or are even poor.

Do you rarely pay the bill when you go out for dinner with your family, splitting it exactly evenly? Do you turn the thermostat way down in the winter time and keep it way up in the summer time to save on your oil or gas bill? Maybe you've done what Sandy Forster's father did. As she described in *How To Be Wildly Wealthy Fast*, when she was young, her family lived on a big hill. Her dad used to coast down it every morning while driving her to school. He would turn the car off at red lights, even when the machine was old enough that it was not clear whether it would restart!

As Mike describes, all these actions are reflections of scarcity—a poverty consciousness—and our "inability to have and do all you want to have and do."

In Christy Whitman's best seller, *Quantum Success*, she reiterates Mike's concept that we were born abundant or prosperous, just like the Universe. She challenges us by asking us to consider how infinite it really is. Consider that there are "more than two hundred billion stars in the Milky Way galaxy, which is just one in hundreds of millions of galaxies ... In the next sixty seconds, the sun will generate enough solar power to fulfill the energy needs of our entire planet for a year." Abundance is our true state of being!

So, what is going on when you are feeling lack, struggle, frustration, or disappointment? Christy says we are just aligning ourselves "with some belief in scarcity ... remind yourself of your decision to remain tuned to your own ... channel, and there is no limit to the abundance available to you ... and to challenge yourself to take on a more generous viewpoint." She explains that by doing this "you will open up a bandwidth for new ideas, impulses, and inspirations to flow in that were simply not accessible to you previously. Your work is to fall in love with the sensation of each of your desired outcomes having already been realized ... and to allow these feelings ... to inspire new ideas within you."

Here is a short story from a woman I met at one of my Rotary Club speeches:

"My family was on vacation in Lake George. We were having dinner in one of the nicest restaurants, the Montcalm. My brother Rocky was eight years old, and he asked my dad if he could order from the adult menu instead of the children's. My dad agreed that he had a bigger appetite than the children's menu could handle and said 'sure.'

"When the waiter came over, my brother ordered 'surf and turf' since his two favorite foods were steak and lobster. At the time, in 1970, the price of the meal was twenty-eight dollars. This was—by far—the most expensive item on the menu. The waiter looked over to my dad who smiled and gave a nod. The waiter left, and I waited for my dad to say something. He went back to asking how we liked our day on the boat. My mother, on the other hand, looked at my brother and said: 'from now on, you're back to the children's menu until you can act like an adult.'

"We all thought she had lost her mind, and my dad laughed it off as her being cheap. The next day we learned that my dad had to work a whole day to bring home twenty-eight dollars."

What does this story bring to mind for you?

Was this child's mom right?

Who was *acting as if?*'

Who was acting from a perspective of lack and scarcity?

For me, how you answer these questions will tell me if you are primed for financial freedom or expect to be working hard your whole life. For me, the ultimate punch line is that the woman who sent me the story is living in abundance and prosperity, and her parents lived an abundant life years into the future.

What is your first money memory?

Take a few minutes now to close the book and get out a notebook and write it down. If you have a partner, tell her or him to write theirs down.

One of my earliest memories was sitting in my grandparents' house with my Uncle David. I was no older than five. He was showing me all of his coin collection. He had traveled all over the world, and the coins he had were all different sizes and shapes and colors!

It was just so interesting and exciting for a young child to see different currencies. To me, they represented all the different people of the world. And they really got me thinking toward learning about all these different cultures. Were they really all that different? What were their similarities?

This experience created a burning desire to visit all these countries and see for myself ...

By knowing that you create your life and taking responsibility for all of it, you can change your beliefs to be empowering ones that will actually work for you, not against you.

But Joel, you say, "Can't I lose all my money in this investment?"

This is a question I get a lot. It could be about cryptocurrencies, a stock, or an option contract. There are many investments where the risk of losing all your money is not zero; think about it. If it is very high—say, more than 25 percent—then you need to decide what your risk tolerance is. If you absolutely need the money to live on, you should not be investing.

Another important point to make here is to focus on what you want, not what you don't want. Go ahead and reread this chapter again if needed, to determine what your belief system is. If for every investment you make, you are focused on the downside, then the likelihood of you losing money is much, much higher, in my opinion. If you spend your days worrying, being fearful and anxious about the potential loss, then what you focus on, you will likely get. And you are far more likely to experience loss.

So focus on the likelihood of the investment going up, not down; focus on the probability of making money, not losing money. What is the chance of making 100 percent or more on this investment?

"You are behaving as a fool if you look outside of you for an explanation of how you should feel or what you should do. Taking credit as well as responsibility for yourself is the first step in eliminating this erroneous zone. Be your own hero." — Wayne Dyer, *Your Erroneous Zones*

Key Points from Chapter 2:

- What are your limiting beliefs? Write them all down.

- What are your empowering beliefs? Write those down.

- The three-step process for installing new beliefs according to Dooley is: "1. Choose beliefs that serve your life. 2. Choose these beliefs through your thoughts and words. 3. 'Act As If' these beliefs are already true every day."

- *Act as if* you are rich and you will be. I acted as if we already had the money to invest for my hedge fund, and we soon did!

- *Act as if* in at least one aspect of your life. Start today!

3

Choose Faith over Fear

"Do one thing every day that scares you" — Eleanor Roosevelt

Let's discuss faith.

The blood was dripping down my face. I ran to the hall bathroom to get a washcloth to stop the bleeding. It was getting in my eyes and running down my cheeks onto my new blue shirt, the one I had worn to the first day of school just a few weeks ago.

I pressed the washcloth to my forehead, as I tilted my head back a bit. After the first washcloth was soaked in the blood, I threw it in the sink and got a second one. It finally looked like the bleeding was slowing, which is when I looked at my forehead. I saw a quarter-inch gash in my head, but it looked okay. And I felt fine. I wasn't dizzy or losing consciousness.

But then the bleeding started again. I grabbed a third washcloth. I remembered hearing something about how cold would stop bleeding. So, I put some ice cubes in another washcloth to try to stop the bleeding again.

I didn't want my mom to know what had happened. I then took the first two washcloths, soaked them in the sink, and then threw them in the hamper—the bottom of the hamper.

I went back to my room and held the ice-filled washcloth to my head and then noticed my new shirt had blood stains. I quickly changed my shirt and threw that in the bottom of the hamper.

I noticed the time was 5:30 p.m. It was a Thursday afternoon. My mom wouldn't be home from tennis for another thirty minutes.

I was a "latchkey kid." My sister usually arrived home first. She was sixteen. I was not yet twelve at the time. I had spent the summer watching the Montreal Summer Olympics on television. I had been particularly intrigued by the gymnastics competition. I was enthralled by Nadia Comaneci who had scored perfect 10s on the balance beam and uneven bars, but her floor routine was what had me mesmerized.

Here I was a few weeks later, having completed my homework early and there was no television in my room. I came up with a game to try to match Nadia. I would run from the hallway, jump onto my bed and try to land on my feet. I was actually getting pretty good at it—coming closer and closer to flipping and landing on my feet. About 5:15 p.m. I did a run, jumped, hit my bed and flipped. Unfortunately, my desk stopped my forward momentum before my feet landed on the ground. Ouch. My desk embraced my forehead directly.

I really didn't feel a lot of pain. Though maybe I was in shock!? There was the blood on my shirt and then the gushing came.

After getting the blood to stop by using the ice, I went back to the bathroom, found a couple of Band-Aids, and put them across the gash. I then covered them with my ample hair so that my mom wouldn't notice.

A reader might ask: "Where was my sixteen-year-old sister?" Well, she was in her room listening to one of her favorite bands, AC/DC. She didn't hear any of what was going on. In fact, like most teenagers, my sister kept to herself most days from the moment she got home until dinner, and then again until the time she went to sleep.

I obviously was happy to not have her know my predicament and even happier I didn't have to bribe her to not tell our mom what had happened.

My mom got home right at 6:00 p.m. She asked me how my day was. I answered "good" as usual.

But when she walked into the bathroom, she noticed a few drops of blood still in the sink and even some on the floor.

So, she started to ask me what had happened, when she saw a Band-Aid which was not completely covered by my hair.

"What is that?" she asked.

"Oh, I bumped my head," I said.

"Can I take a look?" she asked as she came over to me.

I said, "it's nothing."

But when she slowly removed the first Band-Aid, she shrieked—"Oh my God."

"We have to go to the hospital! You need stitches!" She exclaimed.

We sped off to the hospital. Luckily, a plastic surgeon was there. And not only did I get twenty-four stitches, but I also got an expert to conceal the scar.

To this day, no one can tell the line across my forehead is because of an accident and not just aging!

What lessons can be learned from this accident?

First, I had a lot of courage at just twelve years old—I didn't cry. I didn't feel sorry for myself. There was no self-pity. I already had the intestinal fortitude to deal with an accident as if I were an adult. I had faith that everything would be okay. I believed everything would be just fine—and it was.

When something goes 'wrong,' don't panic. See what lessons there are in the situation for you to learn. You don't have to get emotional or upset, because usually this hampers (no pun intended) your ability to see clearly.

Let's discuss fear.

I was in a headlock on the Tucks' lawn. My face was pushed into the grass and I could barely breathe. How did I get into this predicament? I thought they were my friends!

A few minutes earlier, one of my neighborhood buddies—Timothy—the boy I had known since we moved in when I was four, just nine short years earlier, had rung my bell to ask me to go out and play.

I sensed something wasn't quite right. We hadn't really played together since the summertime, weeks earlier, but I was glad to get out and stop doing seventh-grade history. I joined him, walking toward his house, when I was ambushed. The eight grader I had tripped two days earlier in school—sending all his books flying down the hall—was right behind me and jumped me. Though it was an accident, he immediately thought I had done it on purpose, and there was no explaining my way out of it.

It was no contest. I was small for my age. (I would actually grow more inches taller in freshman year in college than in all of high school and junior high). I was on the ground in seconds and here we were. After screaming for what seemed like ten minutes for him to get off, my mom heard me and came running. The bloody nose was the least of my problems.

I'm not sure to this day what was worse: the pain caused by my best friends in the whole world serving me up to someone else, or the humiliation I was going to face by having to deal with them every single day for the next five years, on the bus headed to junior high, and later, walking to high school.

My general attitude toward the world after that incident changed. I began to believe: "People are generally mean; people are not to be trusted, and people can be ruthless." I literally went years without talking to the group on my block; there were three guys in my grade and another three one year older. All became sworn enemies, and whoever became friendly with them were as well.

It took me many years to *know* that not all people are mean, and to know there are some kind souls out there who can be trusted and can actually be helpful.

Can you think back to any incidents in your life that shaped your views of others?

Shaped your view about money? About the stock market? About investing in general?

Here is another story about fear and some key lessons I learned from this experience:

I was shaking with fear and could barely dial the number of my mother's school with my fingers. There were no cell phones in those days, and I literally had to dial on a rotary phone, each number from the school's telephone number that was on a list next to the phone. My hands were actually dripping with sweat, though it was a beautiful, early spring day and the temperature was in the 60s.

I waited patiently, well not really, for my mom to get on the phone. I heard, "Mrs. Salomon, please come to the principal's office as soon as possible" over the loudspeaker in her school. My mom was a reading teacher and helped those who had literacy challenges. She worked about twenty minutes from home. So, I called her first since she was closer and less likely to get upset at me. It was lunchtime, well, actually just 11:49 a.m. I went home for lunch most days in high school. It was fun to make your own lunch or have it waiting for you. It was probably also healthier for me, but I didn't know it at the time. The walk home from school was twelve minutes, but if I jogged or took my secret shortcut, I could make it in six to seven minutes.

On this morning I wasn't in a rush—no exams today—so I had just walked fast. I was thinking about starting work at Nathans soon. I was sixteen and my sister had worked there during her years at secretarial school. I was a shoo-in to get the job since they loved her there.

I just was a little worried about getting all my homework done and working there two nights a week. But I knew the money would be really helpful toward my goal of paying one year's worth of tuition as my dad had asked me to do for going to a private school.

Something seemed off when I got close to my house. There was a car parked across the street on the curve, which was definitely risky. Also, it was rare that any cars were around at midday. All the parents I knew, worked, or they didn't have an extra car.

As I came in view of the house, I saw the front door was ajar. It looked just slightly cracked, but when I got closer, I realized that it was definitely open. How could that be? Then my stomach got this really bad sinking feeling in it. I felt like I was going to throw up.

My mind returned to July 4, 1976. It was already almost four years later, but the memory was burned into me like it was yesterday.

My family and I had returned from a cousin's really fun party. We had watched the Macy's fireworks on TV and I'd had plenty of time to swim in the pool with the cousins. It was such a great day ... not.

When we arrived home, our house was completely ransacked. Furniture was overturned, the televisions were gone, and all my mom's jewelry was stolen. It was close to 10:00 p.m. when we got home, and the policemen didn't leave until almost midnight. They assured us they would find the robbers, but they didn't.

Fast forward to this, our second home invasion, and my mom is now finally on the phone, saying, "I'll be home soon. I'm going to call nine-one-one. If the police get there before I do, just tell them exactly what happened."

"Okay"

Yes, we had been robbed again. But this time I had actually 'caught' them. I opened the door to see a guy coming down the stairs. When he saw me, he shouted something and then starting running. My first instinct was to chase. So I did. I ran after them through the laundry room but they were fast and already out the back door. As I made my way to the back, I saw the second guy jump over our fence into the woods. I stopped my chase then.

Was I sweating so profusely from fear, or did I really run that fast? To this day, I'm not entirely sure, but the next thing I remember, the police and my mom arrived at about the same time. And the questioning began. I didn't really got a good look at them, but they were much older. Twenty-five? Thirty? Not more than that. They ran fast. Again, no one was ever arrested.

What are some lessons learned from this robbery?

I definitely had courage. I had literally chased the robbers out of our house and off our property. For months and years after, I was told I was crazy—by both family and friends.

"They could have had a gun."

"Do you realize you put your life at risk?"

"Why would you chase them?"

I guess I really didn't think. I just acted. And in these instances, instinct just takes over.

A negative belief came out of this robbery as well though. I started to believe that there were more evil people in the world than good ones. This, along with the fight that I had in seventh grade solidified my view of the world and the people in it for at least the next thirty years.

There's an old story about two travelers exploring, hundreds of years ago. Finally, after weeks of movement, they arrive at the gate of a city. They agree that they will approach individually. The first man knocks on the gate, and an old, wise man appears. The traveler asks, "What kind of people live in this city?" The sage responds, "Well, what kind of people are in your city?"

"Well, they are mean and selfish," the traveler responds.

The old man answers with "Well, those are the people you will find here."

Then, the second traveler approaches the gate and asks the same question: "What kind of people live here?" And the sage answers similarly, "Well, what kind of people live where you are?"

The second traveler responds, "My townspeople are kind and generous."

And, of course, the old man responds: "Well, that is the kind of people you will find here."

Clearly, your beliefs and expectations do shape your life.

What you expect does come into your reality. And for years now, I have been expecting the best in people.

But what is fear?

According to the Merriam-Webster Dictionary, *fear* is defined as an unpleasant, often strong emotion caused by anticipation or awareness of danger; an anxious concern. Interestingly, the third level defines fear as a profound reverence and awe, especially toward God.

Clearly a lot of people associate both fear and faith with religion. Of course, as those of you who read *Mindful Money Management* know, I consider myself spiritual, not religious.

"What's your faith?" was a common saying in the 1980s. And it referred to religion. That is not what I mean, of course.

Most people have a lot more fear than faith, especially when it comes to investing.

Why?

Maybe it is because they have not done their homework. Possibly it's because they have not researched the company or companies they are invested in. Maybe it came from your parents who were children of the Great Depression and had to endure days when it was not clear there was going to be food on the dinner table. Or perhaps you lived through the Great Recession of 2008 yourself and your investment portfolio dropped 40 percent or more that year, or your house value depreciated more than 25 percent.

Fear of loss is the biggest stumbling block to success. Fear of taking action because you are afraid you might lose money rather than having the mindset of "This is the best buying opportunity out there," or "I can definitely make money in this investment." Or saying, "Lucrative opportunities always come my way." You can find author T. Harv Eker's, #1 *New York Times* best-selling *Secrets of The Millionaire Mind*™ recommended declarations on my website here: https://www.salaurmor.com/manifesting/

I talked a little about fear of loss in my best seller, *Mindful Money Management*. When I was managing my hedge fund in 2014, there were many days in a row that I lost money. After a while, I actually woke up assuming I was going to lose money. Wow, what a terrible way to live your life. Also, I had a fear of taking action, since I had this thought ("thoughts are things") that if I took action, I was going to lose even more money.

As Napoleon Hill said, "No man who fears anything is a free man."

Fear is really the opposite of faith and believing (Rule #1). It is the belief that you are going to perform poorly or worse. Fear can be debilitating and even lead to death.

There is a famous story of the hazing done by university students back in the early 1900s which I also told in *Mindful Money Management*. The freshmen were being initiated by the juniors and seniors. One freshman was blindfolded and brought to a train depot. There, he was tied securely to the train tracks.

Soon a train sounded its horn miles in the distance. The juniors and seniors left the young man explaining he had to get loose or he was going to get hit.

The upperclassmen had strapped the freshman to a track that was not in use, of course. But when they returned after the train had passed by on the other track, they found the freshman dead. Unable to get free, the young man was literally frightened to death.

His fear had stopped his heart!

What hidden fears do you have? A lot of getting over fear is doing what you are afraid of.

It's early 1987. I had moved out of my parent's house five months earlier. I had rented a basement apartment in East Meadow on Long Island in New York. I was so excited—I was finally independent! I would drive to the train station myself and get home whenever I wanted. I was even able to study for actuarial exams at home. But then sometimes I got to the apartment and the father upstairs was already home from work. He was a policeman and had 'odd' hours. Some weekday nights I finished my bowling league at midnight and got home to hear him hammering away on some repair job in their house. Didn't his kids have to go to sleep for school?

One day I decided to study for the actuarial exam at my apartment. I worked my usual half day and then took a 12:40 p.m. train from Penn Station. Arriving at 1:25 p.m. in front of my apartment in the house where I lived, I parked, and saw the owners' Rottweiler out front. It normally was in the back on its leash and far enough away from the entrance that I didn't have to worry about his barking becoming anything more than that.

I didn't realize that his leash was a long one. I got out of the car and walked toward the back where the apartment entrance was. Unfortunately, this ferocious dog had other plans and he immediately started barking and running at me. I froze. And within seconds he had gotten me to the ground and was on top of me as I covered my face screaming. I remember him going for my throat just as the owner of the house ran to get him off me. Her first response was "What are you doing home so early? Don't you have work?" I think I was still in shock when I responded "I'm fine. He didn't bite through the skin."

I cleaned myself up in my apartment; my suit had some blood on it, but luckily not much. The incident itself was not a big deal. The bigger issue was my fear. From that day forward, I assumed that dog was going to attack me.

And I also assumed every other dog out there would too.

My fear was intense!

And whenever any dog started barking, I usually bolted for my car or the nearest house or store.

Yes, it was irrational.

But don't tell a young man who was recently attacked. And of course, when I recounted the attack to friends and family, they immediately told me how lucky I was to be alive!

Well, that certainly didn't help my fear.

And what did I assume from then on—at least for another fifteen years?

I surmised that dogs were ferocious animals capable of killing me. Yes, even poodles.

I stayed away from dogs as much as possible.

That is, until I made a conscious effort to consider the fact that this was one dog. In fact, my parents had purchased a dog for my sister when she was thirteen that I took care of most of the time. Shaggy was a Pekingese poodle whom I adored and cried over when she passed away twelve years later.

So, I wasn't always this way. And I knew I could change.

In the last ten years, I have.

I consciously made an effort to say in my mind whenever I see a dog, "Nice doggie" and "I love you." In fact, I have seen many loose dogs running around Crawford Park in Rye Brook, New York the last ten years. They've actually come up to me to pet them, which I always oblige. Do they know what I am thinking?

Let's fast-forward to when I was managing money in 2014.

I myself had many a fearful day during this period. There were some times when I had done the analysis, found what looked like a great stock idea, but was unable to make the investment—or—take action!

This happens to many portfolio managers, but it is not talked about often. Living in fear is being scared of making a mistake and thus missing out on opportunities by not taking action. There were many days during the first half of 2014 when I failed to take advantage of mispriced securities because of this fear.

Everyone can be hopeful or be fearful. I was clearly not hoping for the best. I was not hoping or believing that my top stock ideas were going to work—I was worried they wouldn't!

What can you do to stop these feelings of fear?

Start with doing things that are not fearful to build momentum in your belief and having faith.

It can be a small exercise.

Do you believe in your ability to write an article or a blog? If yes, then do that.

If you believe in your ability to do a presentation, then do that.

Maybe you believe in your ability to sing, dance, draw, or paint—do that!

Start with something small. You will build your confidence and have faith that you can do bigger and bigger things.

Let's talk more about how fear plays a big part in investing. We have been taught by almost all financial services companies that as you get older, you should invest less in stocks and more in so-called less risky investments like bonds or cash.

First of all, how is 'less risky' defined? Usually, risk is defined by the volatility of the asset. How much it goes up or down in a particular period, a day or a month, a quarter or a year.

But shouldn't it be defined as the risk of loss—the downside risk? Should we really care about 'upside risk'?

What is the probability of loss in bonds over the next five years (from 2019) given where the ten-year Treasury note is (approximately 2.5 percent)? Well, in the last thirty years, there have only been eight in which the note ended below 3 percent. That is an incredibly low 27 percent chance if we assume that the next five years are similar to the last thirty. But will they be, given that all those eight times took place since the financial crisis in 2008 when the United States Federal Reserve was not increasing the Fed Funds rate like it was in 2018?

If the next five are anything like the time period before the financial crisis, then the probability of the ten-year Treasury note being higher is more than the 73 percent (1–27 percent). And the chance of you losing money in treasury bonds or corporate bonds, which tend to follow the moves in treasuries, is quite high—probably at least two out of three—or more than 66 percent.

Now, given that you know this, why would you "diversify" into an asset class that you *know* has a very high probability of losing money? When interest rates go up, the value of bonds goes down because you would just buy a new bond with the higher coupon rate rather than own the existing bond that yields less.

You would only invest in bonds if you had fear that you would lose more in other asset classes, like stocks. So, it comes back to fear, and its siblings—worry and doubt!

Now let's discuss why.

Were you taught about bonds and stocks growing up?

What did you learn about investments?

Is "common knowledge" what you've gained from watching the talking heads on CNBC jabber on about investments?

Or is it from what you learned by osmosis via your parents talking to each other while you were growing up?

Or perhaps your friends' parents or your friends themselves?

Here is one story I heard growing up. Maybe you can relate:

Whenever someone ordered a Dr Pepper soda when I was with my parents growing up, my mother would say to my dad: "Remember when your dad had the chance to buy that stock right when it went public? (I assume this was at the IPO, or initial public offering price). That was such a big missed opportunity. What would it be worth now?"

Actually, Dr Pepper went public in 1946 and was taken private in a leveraged buyout in 1984.

The definition of faith, according to Merriam-Webster Dictionary, is allegiance to duty or a person: loyalty; fidelity to one's promises; sincerity of intentions. The second-level definition is belief and trust in and loyalty to God; belief in the traditional doctrines of a religion; a firm belief in something for which there is no proof. And importantly, it is also complete trust or something that is believed with strong conviction.

For me, when I talk about faith, I mean something that is believed with strong conviction (Rule #1). Do you have faith in your investment idea? It is not at all religious. Just as fear has nothing to do with religion.

Some readers will ask what actions does the author take when he is down (yes, it does happen). The first recommendation I would have is to 'doubt the doubt'!

Jordan Peterson, in his powerful International best seller, *12 Rules for Life*, recommends: "If the internal voice makes you doubt the value of your endeavors, or your life or life itself ... perhaps you should stop listening!"

In the 2018 comedy, *I Feel Pretty* starring Amy Schumer, the character Renee, says it best: "When we are little girls, we have all the confidence in the world. We let our bellies hang out and we just dance and play ... and then these things happen that make us question ourselves. Someone says something mean to you on the playground. And then we grow up and you doubt yourself over and over again until you lose all that confidence; all that self-esteem that you started with is gone. But what if we didn't let all those moments get to us? What if we were stronger than that? What if we didn't care about how we looked? Or how we sounded? What if we never lost that little-girl confidence? What if when someone tells us we aren't good or thin or pretty enough, we have the strength and the wisdom to say, 'what I am is better than all that, because what I am is me! I am me! And I am proud to be me ...'"

So, think about some affirmations (see the Appendix) to use to get yourself feeling more confident. "I am proud to be me" works well! You could also use: "I am awesome! I am amazing! I am happy! I am successful!"

For me, I start thinking about what I *do* want rather than what I don't want, but maybe that is why I started feeling sad or depressed in the first place. So, then I go to gratitude as discussed in Chapter 7 (Rule #5).

I ask myself: What am I thankful for? Then I go down the list: Lauren and Morgan; my health; all the supportive friends and family I have in my life;

my career helping others become financially free; having completed all the actuarial exams; having become a Chartered Financial Analyst; and the fact that I made money in 2008.

What are you grateful for? See Chapter 7 for a much fuller discussion on gratitude.

Key Points from Chapter 3:

- Even when things don't seem to be going well, have faith and courage.

- Do a little bit of research on your investments—this doesn't mean five minutes, but it doesn't mean five days at eight hours a day either—and your belief level will be higher.

- Fear is the opposite of having faith. Fear is the belief that something bad is going to happen. It is similar to worry ('negative future planning'). So, think about what you do want rather being fearful about what you don't want to happen.

- Fear can literally cause physical illness or death!

- Fear can cause you to miss out on opportunities. "Lucrative opportunities always come my way" is a great affirmation that T. Harv Eker, #1 *New York Times* best-selling author of *Secrets of The Millionaire Mind*™ recommends.

- What fears do you have about investing? About investing in stocks, real estate, stock options, or futures? About IPOs (initial public offerings) or currencies? Write them down now. Know what could be stopping you from achieving the life of your dreams.

- Have faith in your dreams and desires.

4

Rule #2: Can My Intuition Make Me Money?

"What lies behind us, and what lies before us, are tiny matters to what lies within us" — Ralph Waldo Emerson

"Buy Affiliated Managers Group. The symbol is AMG."

"Why?"

"Just do it! I really don't have to explain, do I? We already own it. We should buy more."

"Okay. I'll tell our trader to just buy it here?"

"Yes. Let's buy a thousand, and when I get in, we can see where it is."

"Done. See you soon."

This is a conversation I had with my analyst at Citi in 2010.

I had been using my intuition since 2008, but this was a whole new level. Let's step back to 2008 and the financial crisis. Before then, I hadn't really explored using my intuition for most of my life, at least not consciously. But I found in 2008, that many times when I had a feeling something was about to happen—with a stock, or in the overall market—it did.

I tried to work on figuring out what stock would jump or decline, but I found it easier to try to feel the overall market movement. See, the market is just a voting machine. If most investors/speculators are fearful, the market is likely to go down. If they are greedy or ecstatic, it is likely to go up.

Most days in 2008—excluding those bear market rallies—the fear was palpable. Not only from my colleagues all around me, but just by watching the tickers on my screen, I really felt that fear.

2008 was the year I learned how to use my intuition, like you would use any other skill—credit analysis, equity analysis, or risk management. As I used it more and more, I became increasingly confident that the decisions I made based on my intuition were good ones.

Some people say intuition is just using all the knowledge you've accumulated in your lifetime. I found my intuition helped me make money, and when I didn't trust it, I tended to make less money or lose it.

So, Rule #2 is: "Use Your Intuition!"

In 2010, I was driving back from Hartford after meeting with a company in an investment bank's office the day before. We had then driven up to Boston to see the hated Red Sox play my beloved Yankees. The investment bank's analyst actually drove us back and forth from Hartford to Boston, so I didn't have to drive.

After, after an almost three-hour drive back from Hartford, I was driving on the West Side Highway in Manhattan when a car cut me off. I did the normal thing I did back then when I was in a rush to get to the office and manage my portfolio.

I started cursing them out.

And then, I don't know why, but I glanced at her license plate. I saw, to my astonishment, a stock symbol: AMG 482 on the car's New York state plate. I stopped myself in mid-breath. What does it mean? Well, my intuition told me: "You do not own enough of this stock. Buy more!"

So, I did.

Many will say intuitive hits like this are very rare. And of course, they were very unusual for me. But I've found as you meditate more, it quiets your mind and opens you up to hear what your inner being is telling you. This sixth sense or intuition is powerful.

As I discussed in *Mindful Money Management: Memoirs of a Hedge Fund Manager*, sometimes it's hard to distinguish between a feeling of foreboding that's based on fear and doubt and a feeling that is truly based on intuition or your gut—your sixth sense. How can you know when you are acting out of fear and doubt rather than a feeling of intuition that something "bad" is going to happen? I recommended going back to meditating and trying to be mindful.

Is it a feeling that makes you feel scared or fearful? Or does this feeling make you feel empowered like you can take advantage of "all the lucrative opportunities the world has to offer?" If it is the former, the feeling is likely not intuition, but just a strong negative emotion which can be overcome by meditating or doing something that makes you happy. However, if meditating doesn't change the feeling and you know you should take action to "take advantage of the opportunity," that is using your intuition.

Since that day in 2010, I've had many intuitive hits. Many came from just staring at the Bloomberg screen. Some came while I was actually writing or analyzing a stock, some while I was in the shower thinking about something completely different, and many from license plates.

So, how can you develop your intuition?

I teach my clients that intuition is just like any other muscle, like your bicep. You have to exercise it to make it stronger. You go to the gym and do curls to develop your biceps (at least I used to!), so why not find ways to develop your intuition?

How do you exercise it?

When you are on the subway platform in Manhattan and there is a local train sitting there but an express is coming, use your intuition to decide which one to take.

Every Thursday morning, I take my daughters to school and every Thursday I am presented with options. I can take the highway or the back roads. Usually my intuition says highway. But one day there was tons of traffic on the highway. I used my intellect and I did not *trust my intuition*. I was driving on the back roads and I looked in the rearview mirror and my heart started pounding when I saw the flashing lights and heard the siren. And because I didn't listen to my intuition, I got a speeding ticket that cost me a hundred and fifty dollars. My daughters still tease me to this day and call me "speedy pants."

Let me give you an investment example using intuition. In 2008, we had shorted American International Group (AIG)—bet that the stock was going to go down. AIG had large exposure to the financial crisis, but we had no idea things were so bad that they were going to have to be bailed out by the US Government. We started shorting it in March, and in May, when they announced they were raising money, my gut (or intuition) was telling me to hold on. But the stock had already fallen from $80 to $50 and my analyst—and my intellect—convinced me to get out. We did! And two days later, it was at $45–down 10 percent—in just two days! We shorted it again at $45 and held on, until it was $12. This generated earnings of about 60 percent, as I trusted my intuition.

Here is a great exercise to help develop your intuition. Go back to a time when you used your gut feel or sixth sense to make a decision. Remember how you were feeling at that moment and the minutes right before the decision. Can you remember any feelings or signs inside your body? Do you remember a voice or an image or a particular emotion? How did it feel to just *know* that it was the right decision?

Now where did the feeling come from? Was it truly from your gut, or was it from your head or heart?

What about your body temperature? Did you feel warm all over or was it a chill or an icy feeling?

Consider all these items, because when you now feel them again you will *know* it is your intuition and you will just go with it.

Use your experience. It can help you in investing. You might feel that there is a great opportunity in a sector of the market like three-dimensional print-ing or some new online company that automates calendar entries. Whatever it is, try to use your intuitive hits to determine if it 'feels' right. You can make money using your intuition. Don't let anyone tell you otherwise.

Going back to 2010, from that summer day when I saw the AMG license plate to just three months later, the stock had jumped 13.5 percent. And, if one takes a longer view, at its peak, AMG had more than doubled in the eight years since I saw the license plate.

License plates have become a part of my life after that first sighting in 2010. In actively looking, I was able to find all kinds of stock symbols, though mostly financial stock ones, which happened to be the sector I specialized in at Citigroup, and the only one I invested in at SaLaurMor Capital.

When I started investing money in 2013 for the high-net-worth indi-viduals and institutions that had entrusted me to manage their money, I started seeing symbols on cars in and around Rye Brook, a suburb of New York City.

That was also the year I purchased Fortegra Financial Corporation (FRF). The company was a hodgepodge of businesses—please excuse my technical term! It was one part insurance agency, essentially a distribution company that gets a fee or commission from the purchaser of the insurance policy. Also included was a warranty business that insured cellphones for loss or damage for a small monthly fee, along with a life and health insurance company.

It was a small company with a market capitalization—the value of the com-pany as determined by investors—of less than five hundred million dollars. I found it on my stock screen in 2013, and it appeared to be quite cheap with upside of at least 30 percent. If things went right, we could make a 30 percent return on our investment. The downside was no more than 10–15 percent, so if things went badly, we would lose 10–15 percent.

These were the kind of ratios we were looking for—an upside-to-downside ratio of at least two times—for which FRF qualified, since it was 30/15 or two times. Seeing at least 30 percent upside, we decided to invest in FRF as part of the initial portfolio we put money in during June of 2013, when we started to invest the assets of those who trusted me with their money.

In early February of 2014, there was one day I saw the same stock symbol on eight different cars. Even if one assumed all the license plates on the cars in Rye Brook and Port Chester (the neighboring town next to Rye Brook) started with the letter "F," the probability of seeing eight FRF license plates would be 1 in 676 to the 7TH power, or virtually impossible.

I had done my analysis and found FRF to be a relatively inexpensive security. In fact, you can find my analysis of FRF from December 2013 here: https://www.salaurmor.com/investing/

The stock was at $8.30 at the time and proceeded to decline to about $7 over the next few months. But we continued to buy more, and in fact, on the days I saw the license plates, we might have bought a bit more than other days.

On one occasion in the spring of 2014, I saw the FRF license plate ten times in one day on almost certainly different vehicles!

On August 12, 2014, FRF was acquired by Tiptree Financial Inc. for $10 per share or $218 million and we enjoyed an almost 40 percent return that day—less than a year after making our initial investment.

Another license plate sighting happened in early 2014 when I noticed the stock symbol, AET (Aetna, Inc.), a very large health maintenance organization (HMO). AET was already in our portfolio as part of a "pair" trade with an HMO short. As part of a financial services-focused hedge fund, an HMO was included in the insurance sector because of its disability business and the services that provided insurance to individuals.

The pair trade hadn't been making much money and we decided to unwind the trade later in 2014 by selling AET and buying back the short. However, because of the license plate sighting, I decided to hold on to a portion of the AET stock. AET did well through the rest of 2014—up 25 percent, but the real gains came post 2014. In fact, someone who had purchased $10,000 worth of AET the day I saw the license plate and held it for four years, would have about $30,000—mostly because of the acquisition of AET by CVS Health Corporation (CVS).

One of the most interesting license plate sightings I had was in early September of 2014 when I visited an insurance company at the Hartford office of Janney Montgomery Scott where their insurance analysts worked. I met with the company and then joined one of their avid Boston Red Sox fans for a game at Fenway Park, despite my aversion to the team, being a die-hard Yankee fan.

After the interesting investor meeting, I jumped into the analyst's own car for our drive to Boston. Upon our arrival at the parking lot, I walked behind his car to see his license plate: SFG 487. SFG was the stock symbol for Stancorp Financial Group, and he was either the lead analyst or the back-up analyst for this stock at that time. I asked him if he knew and I seem to remember his answer being that he didn't. Really?

I remember using my intellect instead of my intuition and checking out its valuation. It's P/E (price/earnings ratio: see Part 2, Chapter 4 for a detailed explanation of this ratio) seemed quite high at the time (the stock was expensive) and so were the other valuation measures.

SFG was trading at $63.49 at the close of the stock market that day. I didn't invest in the stock at SaLaurMor Capital, though of course, I wish I had! Less than one year later, a $10,000 investment in SFG would have been worth $18,100 because Meiji Yasuda Life Insurance Company had announced its intention to purchase SFG for $115 per share or about $5 billion in cash.

In the first quarter of 2016, we sold all the securities in the SaLaurMor Capital hedge fund. But something strange started happening in the spring. Throughout my time at SaLaurMor, and Citi as well, I had been an investor in Allied World Assurance Company Holdings (AWH). And when we shut down the hedge fund, we sold all the shares we owned—as we did for all the other securities. But in April and May, my daughter, Morgan, began playing softball in the local league in Rye as she had done the prior spring.

When I went to her games, I noticed one of the license plates started with AWH. And she had games twice a week. So, I started seeing the license plate twice a week. Then I began seeing it every morning! A car that was parked in Crawford Park every morning also had the same license plate. Then I began seeing it at the train station. These were all different cars. There were some periods in May and June of 2016 that I saw the license plate three times in a day (a probability of 1 in 300 million!).

I started buying the shares back—in my personal account. The stock was quite cheap according to my analysis, at just $35. In fact, it had taken a reserve charge earlier in the year which caused the stock to plummet from approximately $38 to about $30. I was sure it was still an acquisition target—some other company would likely buy it in the next few years—and thus it made sense to buy the shares.

Less than seven months later, on December 18TH, Fairfax Financial Holdings (FFH.CN) announced its intention to acquire AWH for $54. The appreciation in my initial investment was more than 50 percent (an almost 100 percent annualized return).

More recently, I was on a trip to Greece and Dublin and stopped off in London on my back to New York. We had an almost twenty-four-hour layoff and stayed at the K West Hotel. That night, walking to a local Indian restaurant, I noticed not one, but two financial stock license plates—in London!

The first one was a company I have been quite fond of most of my career. The symbol is AEL, and the company is American Equity Life Investment

Holdings Inc. The second was Waddell and Reed (WDR). I already owned AEL, but immediately decided this was an amazing synchronicity that I should take advantage of. It was the evening of the 3rd of July in 2017, so I had to wait two days to actually buy more.

AEL was at $26.75 that morning, and though it had been rallying and had been as low as $22.50 as recently as April, I bought more. In 2018, AEL announced it had received some interest from other companies to buy it. It immediately jumped to $37 and traded near that level until the fourth quarter of 2018 (a 38 percent appreciation in less than a year).

The shares of WDR have not fared quite so well. On July 3rd, they traded at $19 after having jumped more than 18 percent in just a few months. WDR peaked 23 percent higher in about seven months, but I didn't know that day in February 2018 would be the peak. In late 2018, it traded as low as $17. Not great, and I am sure your intuition could do better.

Now, how do I know that a license plate sighting is telling me to buy the stock or short it (bet that the price is going down).

What is my intuition telling me?

If you see a stock symbol on a car license plate, would you buy, or would you short it?

What about doing some basic research as I outlined in Part 2, Chapter 4, *My Proprietary Stock Screen.*

Alternatively, you can use an intuitive test like the Sway Test to see what your higher self is telling you.

Here is how to do the Sway Test: Stand up and ask yourself a question that you know the answer to such as:

"Is the sky blue?"

"Do I weigh 135 lbs?"

"Do I love my children?"

"Do I want to be financially free?"

These are grounding questions. Most people sway forward when they ask themselves a question to which the answer is "Yes."

And then ask yourself some other questions:

"Do I love mushrooms?" (I don't)

"Do I love shoveling snow?"

Once you have asked yourself at least three grounding questions, ask yourself the question:

"Is AEL a great stock to buy?"

Now, I would also recommend taking some action by using Part 2, Chapter 4's proprietary stock screen and the other analytical tools in that chapter to determine if AEL is a great long or a great short.

As an aside, I asked a client over the phone to do this, and we just tried one question I assumed was an easy answer: I asked her: "Do you want to be financially free?" She swayed backward strongly. I then asked her another question to which we knew the answer was yes: "Do you live in Michigan?" She swayed forward strongly this time. Strange, but not. She clearly had some strong limiting beliefs about being worthy of financial freedom. The sway test had worked!

To this day, I still see the FRF license plate around town.

What does it mean to me today now that there is no publicly traded company?

It means to have faith. Have faith in your dreams and desires. For me, even when FRF traded down in the months leading up to that auspicious day of August 12ᵀᴴ in 2004, I had faith. I didn't falter in my view that the stock was worth a *lot* more than the seven dollars or seven dollars and fifty cents it was trading at in early 2014.

Key Points from Chapter 4:

- Go back to a time when you remember using your intuition. How were you feeling at that moment and the minutes leading up to it? What do you remember? What feelings did you have? Were you cold or hot? Do you remember a voice or image or emotion? Consider all this, because when you feel them again, you will know it is your intuition and just go for it.

- Your Intuition is quite strong! Use it consciously at least once a day. The elevator in your building is coming and you have two choices; tap into your intuition without looking at the number of the current floor to decide which one is coming first. This is a game I play with my daughters whenever we are on vacation.

- Trust your intuition. Yes, have faith in it and know that it can and will help you in your investments. You have many years of experience and knowledge that your intuition is based on. It is not "airy-fairy" stuff, as one of my mentors used to say. It actually can help you make money if you use it wisely.

5

Rule #3: Be Happy and Become Financially Free!

"Start thinking happy thoughts and start being happy. Happiness is a feeling state of being. You have your finger on the 'feeling happy' button. Press it now and keep your finger pressed down on it firmly, no matter what is happening around you." — *The Secret*, Rhonda Byrne

I was literally in tears. It was July 1, 2015. After having heard the news, I was sitting on the Metro North train which had just arrived at the Harlem – 125th Street stop on the New Haven line at 7:15 a.m. One of my biggest shorts was about to be acquired for a 30 percent premium. Yes, we were hedged, but we definitely should not have been that day! Having a short acquired and having to buy it back 30 percent higher than you sold it, is not the way to start off your day!

Not only that, but I was short a number of companies in the property and casualty (P&C) industry that were going to go up in sympathy. And I found out a few hours later that even those that had no correlation to this large national insurer, Chubb Corporation (CB), were to jump as well. In fact, a Florida insurance company, that we were short and was less than 2 percent of the size of CB, jumped more than 5 percent that day. To make matters worse, the upward trend in these P&C companies continued on for days.

Why was I in tears? I literally felt pain in my stomach. I felt so sad that I was going to lose all this money for my investors. The people who had entrusted me with their money to manage. The people who believed in me and had given me their hard-earned money to manage for them. I felt like I had let them down. I was sad. I felt like I was not worthy of anything!

As I walked into my office thirty minutes later, I put the song that was playing on my headphones on speaker mode so my colleagues could hear:

"Ooh-oo child, things are going to get easier

Ooh-oo child, things'll get brighter ...

Some day, yeah

We'll get it together and we'll get it all done

Some day

When your head is much lighter ..."

— "Ooh Child" by The Five Stairsteps

I was definitely not feeling happy, but the song made me stop crying. I put on a good calm appearance that day and I did realize that things were going to get brighter and easier eventually.

Being happy (Rule #3) does create more happiness in your life. I did enumerate a number of things that can change your mood in *Mindful Money Management* and explained them in detail. Here I would like to list just a few items. Take what resonates and throw out what doesn't.

1. Listen to uplifting songs. Besides "Ooh Child," I also listened to a number of songs with "Believe" in the title. You can find my favorite songs here: https://www.salaurmor.com/inspiration/#lyrics

2. Use affirmations to change your feelings from negative to positive (I list some affirmations in the Appendix). I have free self-talk audio files here: https://www.salaurmor.com/manifesting/ Scroll down to download them. Many will improve your self-esteem.

3. Read some inspiring books. I have my favorites here: https://www.salaurmor.com/inspiration/#books And I give everyone who wants one, a free copy of my now second favorite book, *Think and Grow Rich*, by Napoleon Hill. Contact me on https://www.salaurmor.com/ to get your

free copy. This is the book that changed my life and I have now read it over twenty times.

4. Giving. I will explore this a lot more in Chapter 7, but I found that being of service to others (Chapter 1 in *Mindful Money Management*) was part of my true purpose in life. When I helped others, it not only assisted them, but also made me happier!

5. Meditate. Clearing the mind opens you up to all possibilities (Mike Dooley would say *Infinite Possibilities*). This was Chapter 9 of *Mindful Money Management.*

6. Tapping. Using the Emotional Freedom Technique (EFT) I described in *Mindful Money Management* can literally change your negative energy to positive energy in just minutes. Tapping on key chakra points around the body will actually release your negative energy and allow the positive to flow in.

7. Have fun! Do activities that you enjoy: play a game of ping pong with a friend, play video games, go for a hike or a walk on a sun-drenched day, jog or work out at a fitness center, or get a massage or manicure/pedicure.

As Jeff Olson states in his spellbinding best seller, *The Slight Edge*, "Happy habits don't just make you happier. They also create exactly the attitude you need to make that synaptic leap from the slight edge philosophy to slight edge actions. In other words, those actions start working for you … put the slight edge philosophy together with happy habits, and before long all the other how-to's start working in your life, too."

Jeff then goes on to cite Shawn Achor, the author of *The Happiness Advantage,* the happiness researcher and author he has worked with the most. He explains that Shawn teaches a set of five simple things anyone can do that will make you significantly more happy. Interestingly enough, not having read Shawn or Jeff's book before writing *Mindful Money Management: Memoirs of a Hedge Fund Manager,* I recommended many of the same habits. Jeff suggests the following:

1. **Writing down three things you're grateful for every day**. In *Mindful Money Management*, I discuss the importance of gratitude and even have a whole chapter dedicated to it: Chapter 6 (Being Grateful). In that chapter, I discussed my gratitude journal that I started in 2012 and how what you write down is not as important as the feeling you attach to it when you write it down. You can write down something as simple as "I am grateful for a sunny day." But if you just write it without feeling the gratitude or happiness for it, it is not helpful. We'll talk a lot more about gratitude in Chapter 7.

2. **Journaling for five minutes about one positive experience you've had in the last twenty-four hours**. Journaling is not something I mentioned in *Mindful Money Management,* but I actually do write every morning, after having read *The Artist's Way* by Julia Cameron in 2016. I recommend not only writing about positive experiences, but also just do a "stream of consciousness" in which you write down whatever comes to you. Many mornings I have written negative items. To me, it is helpful to get it out of my head onto paper so that I can stop thinking about them the rest of the day!

3. **Meditate daily**. See #5 above.

4. **Do a random act of kindness over the course of each day**. In Chapter 8 (Happiness) of *Mindful Money Management*, I discuss the fact that Sandy Forster's powerful book, *How to Be Wildly Wealthy Fast*, recommends doing five nice things a day, which I started doing in 2012.

5. **Exercise for fifteen minutes daily**. I also recommended getting outside in Chapter 13 (Feel Good Now) of *Mindful Money Management* to feel the sun's ultraviolet rays—even when there is snow on the ground or even if it is raining—you'll get them anyway! Readers who know me well, know the story I tell about how I started jogging after my first divorce in 1993. I started with a goal to run around my condominium complex

in Commack, New York, since the first run didn't go that well. I lasted about three minutes before I was wheezing and huffing and puffing and trying, unsuccessfully, to catch my breath. But I took baby steps, as Mike Dooley suggests. I ran the next day and went just a little farther, and within a month I had, believe it or not, jogged one mile. Today, I jog almost every day, and in 2018, I logged more than fifteen hundred miles including my longest treadmill experience ever—over six miles while on a cruise ship floating in Glacier Bay, Alaska. In fact, during 2017 and 2018, I walked and jogged more than fifty-five hundred miles—the distance of the Great Wall of China (a picture of which is on my vision board).

Andy Dooley, Mike's brother, says, "Your situation won't get better until you feel better about your situation." What he means is "Feel Good Now!" Don't wait until the manifestation happens. Don't wait until your thought becomes a thing. Don't wait for your dream or desire to come into physical reality. Feel good right now. *Act as if* what you want to happen already happened. Feel the feeling of happiness, and guess what? More and more things will come into your life to be happy about.

So, how can happiness help you become financially free (Rule #3)?

The key is exactly what Jeff Olson states: "Success does not lead to happiness, it's the other way around: more happiness creates more success."

This is true because of the Law of Attraction, which states that you are an energy source and a transmitter and receptor for that energy. When you put out a vibration of the highest level which includes joy, gratitude, appreciation, love, and of course, happiness, you attract those high-level feelings into your life. When you vibrate happiness, you attract more happiness into your life. What makes you happy? More money? More financial success in your investments?

I believe most of you are shaking your head yes right now. That is why happiness is one of the keys to financial freedom.

Oh, and by the way, my hedge fund was up 2.8 percent in August and September of 2015 compared to the common stock market index, the S&P

500, which collapsed 8.8 percent. Those two months were our best relative outperformance while I was managing the fund. A coincidence because of my happiness techniques? I don't believe in coincidences!

In *The Slight Edge*, Jeff cites research that people who see "opportunities instead of problems, who focus on the best in a situation rather than the worst, who notice other people's better qualities and look past their weaker ones, who see the glass, as at least half full ... are happier, more creative, earn more money ... and are more successful in their careers."

I'm going to end Chapter 5 with a great story about how different people define success from Courtney Carver's inspirational book, *Soulful Simplicity*:

"An American investment banker was at the pier of a small coastal Mexican village when a small boat with one fisherman docked. Inside the small boat were several large yellowfin tuna. The American complimented the Mexican on the quality of his fish and asked how long it took to catch them.

The Mexican replied, 'only a little while.' The American then asked why didn't he stay out longer and catch more fish? The Mexican said he had enough to support his family's immediate needs. The American then asked, 'but what do you do with the rest of your time?'

The Mexican fisherman said, 'I sleep late, fish a little, play with my children, take siestas with my wife, Maria, stroll into the village each evening where I sip wine, and play guitar with my amigos. I have a full and busy life.'

The American scoffed, 'I am a Harvard MBA and could help you. You should spend more time fishing and with the proceeds, buy a bigger boat. With the proceeds from the bigger boat, you could buy several boats; eventually you would have a fleet of fishing boats. Instead of selling your catch to a middleman, you would sell directly to the processor, eventually opening your own cannery. You would control the product, processing, and distribution. You would need to leave this small coastal fishing village and move to Mexico City, then LA and eventually New York City, where you will run your expanding enterprise.'

The Mexican fisherman asked, 'But, how long will this all take?'

To which the American replied, 'fifteen to twenty years.'

'But what then?' asked the Mexican.

The American laughed and said, 'That's the best part. When the time is right, you would announce an initial public offering (IPO) and sell your company stock to the public and become very rich; you would make millions!'

'Millions – then what?'

The American said, "Then you would retire. Move to a small coastal fishing village where you would sleep late, fish a little, play with your kids, take siestas with your wife, then stroll to the village in the evenings where you could sip wine and play your guitar with your amigos."

What will it take for you to be happy? Are you already rich today and you don't know it? Rich, that is, in terms of the family and friends you have to enjoy life with.

Key Points from Chapter 5:

- You can create your own happiness. What are your happy habits? Write them all down. And be prepared. Know which one(s) you will use when you inevitably have an emotion that is not one of the good ones like happiness, joy, passion, or ecstasy. Then practice your go-to habit before you actually feel unhappy.

- Being happy does cause more happy events to come in to your life.

- Some techniques to create unconditional happiness in your life could include: listening to uplifting songs, saying affirmations, reading inspiring books, giving to your favorite charity, meditating and playing games.

- Remember Shawn's five tips: write down three things you are grateful for each day, journal for five minutes, meditate daily, do one random act of kindness every day, and exercise.

6

Rule #4: What does Visualizing have to do with Money?

"You are a divine creator today; a spiritual being. You don't need anyone to tell you that!" — Wayne Dyer

The Sermon on the Mount

Ask and it shall be given to you; seek and you shall find. Knock, and it shall be opened for you. For everyone who asks, receives; the one who seeketh, findeth, and to the one who knocks, the door will be opened.

One of the items I didn't enumerate in *Mindful Money Management* was creative visualization. This is actually Rule #4! This is a happy habit that can quickly get you to be ecstatic. The first step is to find a comfortable place where you will do it every day. Then schedule the time to do it. The next step is to write down three dreams or desires that you will consciously think about each time you sit down to visualize. And the most important step is to feel the feelings and emotions of the dream or desire actually occurring. I recommend visualizing for at least three and no more than five minutes each day.

And it would be even better if you could see yourself in the "dream." Try to be as specific as possible when you visualize. If your dream is to go on vacation to Fiji, then picture yourself in the bathing suit on the beach with the sun beaming down on you. Really feel the warmth of the sun. If you like swimming or snorkeling, imagine having your flippers and mask on, being in the turquoise water, seeing the amazing blue-and-yellow regal angelfish.

Christy Whitman, in her best seller, *Quantum Success*, specifically enumerates the steps for creating a relationship in the present time with your future self through visualizing. Her first step is: "letting yourself dream as big and as freely as you can … you can begin to conjure an image of the most awesome, fulfilling, successful career … allow yourself to remember and to connect with what you are truly passionate about … energetically connect with that vision." Her second step is to "visualize and imagine a future in which you are engaged in the work that feels powerful, purposeful, and prosperous. Ask your future self to show you images of what your day-to-day life looks like. How many hours do you work per day? How much freedom do you have? Etc. Allow yourself to remember and to connect with what you are truly passionate about." And finally, she says the third step is the believing step: "Expect that the shifts you desire to make are already in the process of unfolding." She explains that when you expect what you want to happen it is like you are "believing that it's possible; believing you are capable of creating it; and believing that you are deserving of having it."

As I stated on my website, https://www.salaurmor.com/manifesting/, the word "manifesting" gets a bad rap. While it's true that manifesting requires belief *and* action, it's also true that your thoughts create the foundation for the "magic" associated with manifesting a prosperous life.

For those who read *Mindful Money Management: Memoirs of a Hedge Fund Manager*, you may remember this story:

"I started reading *The Secret* in 2007, but began focusing on preparing for my new job at Citigroup which I began in January 2008. This was my first job where I was working as a Portfolio Manager and getting paid for my performance. I picked up *The Secret* again in February 2008, and I came to a part that really intrigued me. In the book, it talked about this man who thought about this feather. Not any old feather, but a very unique feather with etchings and carvings and various colors in it. He thought about it day and night, until one day he happened to be walking down the street and saw the feather he had imagined in his mind weeks before.

"In the book it then said, 'You try!' So, I did. I read that passage in February, and the first thing that popped into my mind after reading it was cotton balls. Pure white cotton balls. I don't know why, but that is what popped into my head.

"So, starting in mid-February, I began thinking of cotton balls when I woke up and again right before I went to sleep. Every day—day and night.

"At the time, my daughters, Lauren and Morgan were just four and two, and I had a double jogging stroller that I used to go jogging with them. When it became warm enough in April, I jogged with them around a local high school track and then to Crawford Park in Rye Brook, New York. I ran up the hill and then to the playground. This is where I got my well-deserved five to ten-minute break. I let my little girls out of the stroller and pushed them on the swings and down the slide. Then back into the stroller for the jog back home.

"Well, we did this every Saturday and Sunday when I had them in April and May. And on May 31st, we were doing our usual jog. I had pushed my girls up the big hill, arriving at the playground. I was letting them out of the stroller when I looked down and saw all over that playground, hundreds of cotton balls.

"I was in a state of shock as I screamed at Lauren and Morgan to pick up as many as they could. I had been believing for months that I would see cotton balls and yet when I did finally see them (and of course, not just one or two but tons of them!), I was quite surprised. But once I finally got over the shock, a feeling of joy and bliss came over me. Wow, this does indeed work. It did take some time—over three months in my case—but they did show up!

"For years after, I had a sand-covered cotton ball at my desk at work to remind me that thoughts are indeed 'things.' You can, without a doubt, manifest physical things into reality."

But this is not the full story!

Have you ever wanted something so bad that you worked too hard to get it? Have you ever started feeling doubt about what you wanted?

What I didn't include in *Mindful Money Management: Memoirs of a Hedge Fund Manager,* was that at the end of April 2008, I started to doubt that the cotton balls were coming. After asking for cotton balls, every morning and every night for over two months I gave up ... kind of.

Yes, I stopped thinking about them every morning when I woke up and every night when I went to sleep. When I look back on this manifestation now, I call what I was doing "white knuckling it." Some people say "forcing it." When you ask and ask and ask but don't really believe or have little faith, but ask in a needy way, what you are really doing is putting up resistance to what you want because you are fixated on the fact that you don't have what you are asking for. Asking with ease, with little or no resistance, is a knowing that it's coming. It's like having absolute faith. And when you "let go" or stop focusing on needing the result, that is when you stop focusing on the "lack" or not having what you want, and you just "be." And that is when what you want comes quickly into your life.

For me, I "let go" of the focusing on the cotton balls. I had already asked for them enough!

I had told the Universe what I wanted for over two full months. I had asked. Now, it was my job to just receive—to allow—to know that it was coming and just let go of the resistance. To let go and not "need" the cotton balls. To let go and not force them to come into existence (which doesn't work anyway), but just allow them to come. And lo and behold, on May 31st when I went jogging with my daughters, not one, not two, but tons of cotton balls were on the ground at the playground at Crawford Park in Rye Brook.

So the full picture of getting what you want is to ask and then allow— allow yourself to receive the gift(s) that you asked for a long (or short) time ago.

Most of us ask and ask and ask, and when it's a burning desire, we might actually be focusing on the lack of what we want and then that is when significant resistance is built up.

When you allow, it comes easily.

When you think about what you want and you are feeling happy, joyful, even ecstatic, that is when you know you are on the right track.

In one of Esther and Jerry Hicks' earliest books, *Ask and It is Given*, they talk about the three-step process to "Whatever You Want to Be, Do, or Have (aka Manifesting)."

They say the first step is to ask, then the answer is given, and then the third step is to allow the answer to be received—you have to let it in. And this is where the problem arises!

Step three they call "The Art of Allowing." And they describe it as the step whereby you tune "your vibrational frequency ... to match the vibrational frequency of your desire." They continue by saying that unless you are in the allowing mode, "your questions, even though they have been answered, will seem unanswered to you; your prayers will not seem to be answered, and your desires not fulfilled" because you are not letting your desires in.

Importantly, they continue, "As long as you are more aware of what you do not want regarding the situation, what you do want cannot come to you." That is, if every time you think about a new car, you are thinking about all its beautiful aspects, then it is making its way to you. But if every time you think about your need for a new car, you think about your undependable old car, your new car is *not* coming to you.

In Christy Whitman's inspiring book, *Quantum Success*, she talks about allowing by stating that "the universal law of allowing is based on the understanding that creation is just as much a by-product of the inward ebb as it is the outward flow ... the tide first has to recede in order to gather strength to form into a wave. A seed must first be buried deep into dark soil before it receives the impulse to begin its upward journey toward the sun ... so how does this universe function, then, if not by hard work and willpower? It functions through the simultaneous phenomenon of attraction and allowing ... by becoming more allowing, we become more receptive to the replenishing energies of relaxation, surrender, and peace."

She further explains: "Most of us were taught that if we want to make things happen in our lives, then we need to bring to bear the full force of our focus, conviction, and determination in a kind of 'pedal to the metal' attitude." This is the "white knuckling it" phenomenon I mentioned earlier.

This is how I was raised. And I am pretty sure you were taught this way too.

"You have to work hard to be rich and successful" is a mantra that was embedded in my programming from an early age. The problem is, as Christy says so eloquently, "Too often, under the guise of manifesting our desires, we are actually attempting to control how, when, where, and with whom our desires will be fulfilled." She goes on: "It's great to visualize, daydream, plan and set goals, but at some point, we need to trust that these efforts have already been set into motion and allow things to manifest in their own way and in their own time ... when we surrender our attachment to needing to know how, who, what, when, and where it will happen, and place our attention instead on simply aligning ourselves in heart and mind with the essence of our desire, the universe makes it happen for us." She says that the law of detachment states that "The fastest way to manifest any outcome is to relinquish our attachment to it!"

I truly believe this is what happened when those cotton balls showed up at the playground at Crawford Park in Rye Brook in May 2008.

In *Sapiens*, Yuval Noah Harari discusses the pursuit of happiness. He describes a man standing for decades on the beach, enjoying the "good" waves and trying to stop them from ending, while at the same time pushing the "bad" waves away to stop them from getting to him. He does this day after day after day, obviously driving himself crazy in the task. Eventually, he just sits down on the sand and allows the waves to come and go as they please. And guess what? He finds peace.

Allowing can sometimes seem like you are not doing anything. You are not 'working hard enough.' But if your labor at the end of the day is actually fruitless, wouldn't it be better to just sit there and meditate?

I'm not saying stop taking action; by all means, do so! But taking massive action for the sake of massive action will not get you closer to your goal.

If fact, a common question I get after telling the cotton ball story is:

Do you need to take action to make massive amounts of money?

First of all, this assumes that meditating, visualizing, and focusing is not doing anything. As Abraham Hicks says: "But focus is doing something! Focus is harnessing the energy that creates worlds. The power of your mind is the only power that matters and all the other stuff you do is just for the pleasure of enhancing what you've really done with your mind. And the real power is the focus, and for you to call that nothing could not be further from accurate."

Abraham talks about "tapping into the energy that creates worlds and … (having that flow through) your experience." Abraham goes on to say that, "the people that are working the hardest in terms of action are receiving the least and the people who are working the least are receiving the most. How do you reconcile that? Most don't! Most just say 'that sucks' Most just say: 'that's injustice.' Most just say: 'let's take the pie and split it up again. Let's take the pie and split it up again … And it does not matter how many times you split that pie up: it will move into the vibrational places where law of attraction puts it! In other words, you just can't orchestrate it through action. It is a vibrational attraction or allowance that it is all about."

Abraham continues by saying that people want money to feel better, but in reality what they really want is vibrational alignment and the alignment brings the money. "They want the money so that they can then observe alignment.

And we say they want the alignment, which will bring the money." Abraham concludes by saying: "You've already created it, with all that you've been living! And it's waiting for you, offering a signal and all you have to do is home in on that signal! And you can tell when you're homing in, because you're feeling better! And you can tell when you're really homed in, because you believe! And you can tell when you're consistently homed in, because you know!

"And you just expect it to be good and now you're moving through life … doing the action that supports your knowledge of well-being! (When) you get tuned in, you won't cease to act. We promise you when you're tuned into the energy that creates worlds … the inspiration will flow through you. You'll be the busiest, most active person that you've ever known in your life. But the inspiration comes first and inspires the action. The action doesn't create!"

I want to describe another process of manifestation that Wayne Dyer recommends in his best seller, *Wishes Fulfilled*. A great quote from that book is "Make your future dream a present reality by assuming the feeling of the wish fulfilled." In this book, which I read in 2016, Wayne recommends getting a cardboard box and writing on all four sides and the top: "Whatever is contained in this box, *is*," which I did. And to me that means that whatever you put in the box exists in the physical world somewhere. Well, I threw in some dream furniture, some dream homes, some dream vacations, and … even a dream car in there. I didn't really look at any of these items closely though.

In January 2018, as I am a Hyatt credit card holder, I received a letter from Hyatt saying that they were doing a promotion for their Maui Residence Inn for just one thousand dollars for six days and five nights. I quickly booked the end of August when I had my daughters for a week or so for summer vacation. Well, I figured since we were going all the way to Maui, we should also go to the Big Island to tour the rainforest and the Volcano (this was before it had begun to spew lava later in 2018).

I went on Travelocity and did a search for hotels from least expensive to most. I don't remember the least expensive, but one of the cheapest ones was called The Sheraton Kona Resort and Spa. I checked it out and it had a nice pool for my daughters who love to swim. So, I booked it for two nights.

A few weeks later, Morgan saw the cardboard box that my cleaning lady happened to move and asked what it was. I explained, and she asked if we could open it and go through it. I said, "Of course, we can." I thought it would be interesting to look at the pictures that I had cut out from all the magazines two years earlier, not really remembering exactly what was in the box.

After going through a number of items, we came upon a postcard (see below) that listed three hotels. The first one was the Sheraton Kona Resort & Spa, and the third one was the Hyatt Regency Maui Resort and Spa. The very two hotels we then visited in August of 2018.

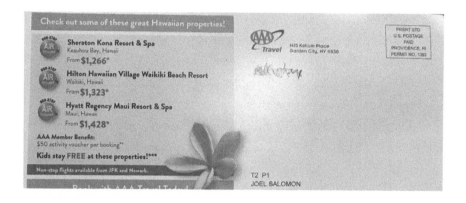

Coincidence? I don't believe in coincidences, only synchronicities.

This is another way that manifestation works.

It is interesting to note that I didn't spend day after day thinking about Hawaii and how I was going to go there on vacation with my daughters. I should note, though, that when I asked them in May of 2017 what vacation(s) would they like to go on in the future, they did say, "Hawaii." Furthermore, I also wrote this sentence on page 200 of *Mindful Money Management: Memoirs of a Hedge Fund Manager* in the summer of 2017:

Maui is a place I am really looking forward to visiting again with Lauren and Morgan, in the near future.

I believe this is an example of a manifestation that happened from asking and allowing with little to no resistance. I had a *knowing* that I would get to Hawaii with my daughters. I didn't know *how* or *why*. But that is the beauty of manifesting. You don't have to know how or why. You should ask and then allow. The Universe does the rest.

An important concept to discuss about manifestation is the time lag between when you want something and when it comes into your physical reality. For Hawaii, the manifestation took over a year from the time I put the postcard in the box.

Why do some things take so much time?

Christy Whitman in her best seller, *Quantum Success*, gives an excellent explanation: "… there is … a lapse of time between the moment we realize we want it and the moment we throw that first pitch or take the first bite … but what is it that determines how long that period of time lasts? … the answer to the question … lies in understanding the difference between dwelling in an attitude of waiting and stepping into the attitude of having … if we deprive ourselves of happiness and satisfaction along the way, pretending that the success we desire will be ours only when we reach some future destination; we trap ourselves in an endless cycle of waiting and wanting that prevents us from ever reaching the promised land of finally having. More importantly, as long as we are waiting for a particular outcome to occur in order to feel happy or successful, we deprive ourselves of the experience of loving the life we have right now. And the secret to getting more of anything you want is to love and appreciate what you already have."

It's back to feeling the feeling of what you want to happen *as if* it has already happened.

Some of you may remember this sentence from *Mindful Money Management*: "As of September 2017, I am just one state short of reaching all fifty (Alaska). As they say in the Broadway hit show *Hamilton*, 'Just you wait ...'"

Here is another story about manifestation and synchronicities.

After I shut down my hedge fund in 2016 and sold all the securities in the first quarter, I decided to get back on Facebook. One Saturday night I was out in Manhattan, and while somewhat bored, I decided to check out the latest "People you may know." I was surprised to see my first girlfriend was one of the recommendations. I hadn't seen Karen in at least ten years, but I remembered that she had been living in Providence, Rhode Island with a guy she had met up there after she had started her amazing non-profit, Young Voices. Well, I figured what the heck! It would be interesting to catch up with her and see if she was married and reconnect. So, I tapped on "Add Friend."

I reached out to her a few days later and asked if she wanted to catch up over the phone. Yes, a real live phone call for those who don't talk on the phone these days!

Well, we did reconnect a few weeks later on a phone call. I wasn't sure exactly how this synchronicity was going to unfold, but I was curious. We started talking about our experiences in life and family over the last decade or so. This went on for over an hour, and we both realized we had other things to do. I'm thinking to myself how this was a really great conversation, but nothing earth-shattering.

Then Karen apologizes for it being so difficult for us to connect, since last weekend she had been at a conference that she goes to most years held by Abraham Hicks. She asked me if I knew about Esther, Jerry, and Abraham, and I said I really didn't. Someone had suggested I read *Ask and It is Given* back in 2012 when I was in a Mastermind Group then, but I had only read a few pages and it really didn't resonate with me at the time.

Well, Karen insisted that I try to read the book again, and that she would also send me a few links to YouTube videos that she found particularly powerful.

Karen sent me three videos. And I remember listening to two of them and just bawling! The first one, called "Everything is always working out for me," is a very uplifting sequence, while "Experience Beingness" is a hot-seat dialogue that goes on for over thirty minutes on the benefits of being present and happy and allowing.

I was hooked.

In fact, in 2019, I was listening to those two YouTubes almost every morning when I went jogging.

Now, you might be curious about the book *Ask and It is Given.* Well, it is now on my website –https://www.salaurmor.com/inspiration/#books–as one of my recommended inspirational books.

With that as background, the following story becomes an incredible synchronicity and manifestation.

In February 2018, one of my clients called me up and asked me if I knew anyone who wanted to go on a cruise.

I asked, "Why?"

She replied that her partner was not well, and although they had already reserved and paid for the cruise, she didn't think it made sense for her partner to go, though she herself still wanted to.

I asked where the cruise was going and she said, "Alaska"! Well, I asked if it was okay if I joined her (she didn't know it was my last state in the union to visit). And she said, "Let me ask my sister first, but if she answers no, then it's yours." She agreed to call me back the following Tuesday, four days later. Well, four days later I was booked on a cruise to Alaska.

And what an even happier surprise it was when she told me that it was an Abraham Hicks cruise. See, I had introduced this client to the teachings of Abraham when I took her on as a client in late 2016. So, it came full circle.

What an amazing manifestation!

Here is the powerful "Oath of Manifestation" by Reverend Dr. Cheryl Ward. I recommend saying it every night before you go to sleep:

"I accept and receive unexpected good, unexpected money, unexpected love, unexpected kindness, unexpected generosity, unexpected offers, unexpected prosperity coming in, unexpected ways from unexpected places in my life and the life of others.

I am constantly guided and boldly empowered, to receive the lavish abundance of the Universe!

I accept the Principle that abundance and prosperity have already been given to me.

My acceptance makes it real and opens the space for manifestation to rush in!

I open wide the doors of my consciousness to receive and to give! It is done now!

Through this 'Oath of Manifestation,' ALL things are possible!

I declare, absolutely, that I live in a friendly Universe that is always providing for me. I feel it powerfully happening now!

I open myself to receive more abundance, and to give more abundance than I have ever experienced before!

I can afford anything I desire! In fact, I am so prosperous I need never worry again!

I am grateful for all that I have had, all that I now have and all that I will have.

And so it is!"

And finally, to conclude this chapter on Manifestation—in 2017, I put together a travel vision board. I cut out pictures from magazines when I found places that I wanted to visit in the future. On that vision board, besides a picture of Hawaii, I also had pictures of The Great Wall of China, the Taj Mahal, an island on the Maldives, Bangkok, The pyramids of Egypt, and a few other places I really wanted to get to.

In April 2018, I was jogging near my house in Rye Brook, New York and I saw a license plate, "I-PERU." I thought that was interesting since I did have Machu Picchu on my vision board, but I didn't think about it again until I received a Note from the Universe later that week reminding all Infinite Possibilities trainers and Mike Dooley fans that he was doing a "WoW" tour to Machu Picchu. I thought, "Wouldn't it be great to go there this year too." I thought about it for a few minutes, but I didn't take any immediate action. I figured I had plenty of time to decide to go since his tour was in October. I thought to myself I'll decide in July or August …

Well, on June 27th, I got an email from Andy Dooley, Mike's brother. I get emails from him almost every week since he is very inspirational and loves to inspire others. To be open with you, I don't normally read them immediately. In fact, I'm not sure if had opened any of them on the day I received them. And I definitely hadn't scrolled through the whole email. But this particular one—for some reason—I decided to open that day.

And not only that, but instead of just watching the video attached, I decided to scroll all the way down since the title of the video was "Gain clarity—3 minute video. Join Mike and me in Peru." And then I saw this: "Registration closing June 30th! Only 5 spots available. Take action today."

What? There was a deadline! And there were only five spots left. OMG! So, I took action. On June 28th, I reserved my space, and then over the next few days, I booked my flights (the group tour flights were already completed booked).

Then, just a week later, the cover of my monthly AAA (American Automobile Association) newsletter that I received in the mail read: "The Senses Take Flight in Peru."

Again, I don't believe in coincidences. There are only synchronicities. And this amazing manifestation took me to another place on my vision board, Machu Picchu!

Here is a story about abundance and manifesting from Julie, an Infinite Possibilities trainer:

"I was about to get divorced and I was really scared. My husband had his own business and had been doing well for many years, but I sensed that something was going to happen. It was really weird. And I was scared and I didn't know if I'd really ever get child support from him.

"I was supposed to get paid every month. I did for two years—at least a few thousand, but my youngest child was eight so I was supposed to get paid for about ten years, but he only paid two. And, after that, he just quit and there was nothing I could do because he went downhill, big time. He lost his business, he went into a big depression. I just let go. I just had to let go and decided I had to figure out a way to make ends meet. I have four kids.

"So, I lived in my office house for six months because we sold our home. I had a lot of time to just visualize my dream life. I had a vision board where I had a high-rise apartment: a picture of a high rise looking over the city. I just really focused on wealth, despite my current circumstances.

"So, the next step was to move into this little Victorian home, where I was trying to grow my business while I was going through divorce. And I just had to have a lot of faith, because it was even scary renting that little Victorian home.

"We get divorced. And I have one month to find somewhere to live. I started to look around and I like nice things. As a designer, working on people's homes, I knew I wouldn't be happy just with a basic apartment.

"During the time I was going through divorce, an old friend of mine found me on an online dating service and asked me out. I just wanted to be friends and eventually he became a dear friend. He took me to his apartment complex in a popular area; he lived in a high rise, and I went there and his apartment was on the 18ᵀᴴ floor. And it had an amazing view. And I thought it would be so nice to live here, but I couldn't get my head around it. *Can I afford this?* This was what my logical mind was saying! But this was on my vision board: an apartment with a view.

"So, my dear friend introduces me to the apartment manager because he knows I'm an interior designer and I also design apartment buildings and condo buildings. The manager was happy to know me, and then right when I started looking for a place to live, I got a call from him. Now, this building is really hard to get into. But he says that there is availability. But I kept on thinking I'm not going to live on a low floor. But he called me and he said he didn't even know I would be interested, and of course, he had no idea about my vision board.

"So he calls me and he says there's one apartment available and do I want to take a look at it? I ask him what floor it's on, and he says '16.' Now I'm thinking that is high up! It was one of those things that just came to me, and then of course, the next question is can I afford this?

"But after I took a look at it, the manager offered me a few hundred dollars off because he really wanted to get me in there, knowing that I was a designer and that they were going to remodel over the next year.

"He gave me a special price and I was able to pick out everything: the paint colors, the special blinds, lighting, and even the carpeting. It was really more like a condo. They let me really customize this two- bedroom, two-bathroom apartment. Then I move in and my business quadruples.

"And … the next year, the apartment manager hired me to design all twenty floors in that building where they purchased all the products from me too. So I trusted my vision board … and the wealth and abundance just flowed."

In Christy Whitman's best seller, *Quantum Success*, she gives us specific steps to be prosperity conscious, which I practice almost every day. Her recommendations include:

"1. Consider the quality of the information you consistently expose yourself to … make a daily practice of reading, listening to and meditating on uplifting messages that encourage and are consistent with the vibration of abundance.

2. Be mindful of your thoughts and words, for these become your reality.

3. Seek out high-minded and like-minded others. Surround yourself with spiritually aware and successful people who express qualities and character traits that you would like to emulate.

4. Give of your time, talents, money and resources—10 percent or more—to causes that call to you or inspire you, and extend generosity to those who contribute to you. Look for opportunities to help others get what they want.

5. Think, walk, stand, speak and behave as though you already are the person you desire to become. Pay attention to posture, dress and the rest of your appearance.

6. Clarify your desired outcome in advance of each important event or interaction and visualize it as having already unfolded brilliantly.

7. Joyfully expect that good and wonderful things are in the process of flowing into your life right now. Look for the blessings, notice them and appreciate them—journal them or give thanks for them daily."

Christy also discusses "forward thinking." She explains that if your mind is not focused on the current physical reality, what is it doing? It is focused on the future possibility, also known as forward thinking. This is just a state of "positive expectation in which we don't concern ourselves with what is, but allow ourselves to lean in body, mind, gut, and spirit—in the direction of what could be … it's allowing ourselves to daydream."

Here is the technique she recommends:

"1. Pick something that you believe is possible for you to have.

2. Be as specific as you can.

3. See how many of your five senses you can recruit toward this end. What does the realization of your objective look like, sound like and taste like?"

Then she recommends using "your imagination to sustain the feeling for a minimum of at least sixty-eight seconds. In your mind and in your gut, play with the feeling of having fulfilled every one of your … goals until this vibration is deeply familiar to you."

She goes on to discuss how you can meet your future self by allowing "yourself to recall an earlier time in your life when you were in the midst of some kind of challenge. Maybe it was a problem you were having with a boss, or a breakdown in a relationship with a family member; anytime in your life when you felt confused, blocked, or unsure about how to proceed. And now imagine that right now you had the ability to go back in time and transmit to that younger version of yourself all the experiences, wisdom, confidence and resourcefulness you now possess. Can you see the younger version of you benefiting from your wiser and broader perspective?"

She clarifies that, "Your future self exists as a wavelength—a particular frequency that you are naturally attracted to because it represents you …"

Whitman explains that when you are early in the process of manifesting you should go general and only focus on the next "logical steps to the life you desire." She recommends not deciding right away what your endgame vision is for your career, or for any aspect of your life. She states that early in the process you might not know.

She also recommends that you "Reflect back over your life and notice the high points, the peak experiences, that easily jump out at you. In which periods of your life did you feel the most inspired or the most connected to your innate strengths and talents? When did you feel that you were making the biggest contribution to those around you? To the extent that you are able, identify the inner qualities that these situations brought to life within you and write them down."

Finally, Whitman explains the specifics that she uses for manifesting:

- "Bring to mind a vision of you—happy, prosperous, and at the top of your game in relation to your career ... What would you have more of or less of if this vision were already fulfilled? Would you have more security, more freedom from worry, a simpler life?

- Now having identified that deeper need or desire, ask yourself what you could do right now, in your present circumstances, to begin to bring more of that feeling into your life. If you're not sure what activities would support you in cultivating your essence feeling, simply begin making a list of everything you can possibly think of doing that would be consistent with that value. If joy is one of your essence qualities, ask yourself: 'What activities bring me the feeling of joy?'

- ... to realize the full manifestation of the success you're looking for, you must learn to focus the power of your mind and emotions to tune in to the plane of existence—to the specific energetic channel—where the essence of that success already exists."

Key Points from Chapter 6:

- There are many ways to create manifestations. Choose at least one of these exercises and do it right now.

  - Create a vision board: Go through your magazines you have around the house or go buy some. Cut out pictures and words that resonate with you. Get glue and a poster board and glue the pictures on the board. Put the poster board some place where you will see it every day (I put mine in my bedroom).

  - Create a vision box. Buy a cardboard box. Write on all four sides and the top of the box: "Whatever is contained in this box, *is*." From the magazines you now have, cut out pictures and words and throw them in your vision box. Put the vision box someplace in your house where you will see it daily. Add to it whenever you see something that you think you would like to have. Open up the box and go through it every year or so. Take out what has manifested and add more of your new dreams and desires.

- Remember to "Ask, Believe," and then "Allow."

- The quickest way to any manifestation is to feel the feeling of the manifestation as if you have already received it. Gratitude is a great emotion to feel before you have received what you ask for because the feeling of gratitude is most often *experienced* after receiving something you asked for.

- Read the "Oath of Manifestation" daily, out loud, preferably right before you go to sleep.

7

Rule #5: What Can You Be Grateful For?

"Random Acts of Kindness happen all the time but they mostly go unseen ...

It is not always front page news, when you do the right thing.

It would be so much easier to walk away, go about my business and live selfishly ..." — Nick Swisher, Believe

To continue the story that began this book, Morgan is at the pediatrician on Monday morning after her temperature was elevated over the weekend...

The pediatrician determined right away that it was a blockage in her urinary tract. And surgery was likely necessary!

What?

Our only question was, "Is there any way to solve this problem without surgery?"

The answer was, "No."

Our fear and worry were off the charts now. Both Christine and I liked to be in control and in this situation we could do nothing. We had to rely on the experts.

We agreed to the surgery which the doctors assured us was a very minor procedure, and she would not even need to stay overnight.

But neither of us were prepared to see our beautiful baby daughter connected to all those wires, and the intravenous tube. And then we watched the Doctor give her the "laughing gas" to put her out, so that she would not feel any pain.

That was the hardest part for me. I couldn't stop the tears from falling as we were forced to leave the room. I felt completely out of control.

I don't remember when I stopped crying. But the Doctor did come out in less than a couple of hours to say the operation was a success and she would be out shortly.

Again, neither of us were prepared to see Morgan still connected to those wires and IV tube when she came out of the operating room. But Morgan was (and is) a strong girl, and within a few hours, the color had returned to her face and she was smiling and happy.

We took her home that night and I remember jumping up at the "normal" 4:00 a.m. time, but not hearing her cry. She no longer needed to be comforted at this time and she slept easily through the night.

I remember those days now with gratitude. Yes, gratitude. I am grateful for how strong Morgan was at that very young age. I am grateful that she made it through the operation with flying colors. I am grateful we went through the experience. Because truly what doesn't kill you makes you stronger. I don't believe in mistakes, or bad vs. good. I believe there are just experiences. And this is one experience in which Christine and I learned a lot about ourselves, as well as learning about how strong and courageous our daughter is.

I am now so grateful for having a very healthy, beautiful, caring, thoughtful, loving, and intelligent daughter. This is Rule #5 (Be Grateful).

And now she asks: "Is that why I have that line on my stomach?"

"What can you be grateful for today? Who can you be grateful for today? Could you even be grateful for some of the problems and pain that you've been through in your life? What if you took on the new belief that everything in life happens for a reason and a purpose, and it serves you? What if you believed in your heart of hearts that life doesn't happen to you, it happens for you?"

— Tony Robbins

"Harold! Harold! Are you okay?"

"Yeah. I think so. Just a bit dazed. Man, what happened? Those fireworks were really loud. And the smoke!"

It was July 4, 1982. It was going to be the best summer of my life. I had just graduated from Berner High School in Massapequa on Long Island, New York. I was only working at Nathans about thirty-five hours a week. But having gotten a raise, I was making more than $140 a week and it would amount to almost $1,400 for the summer. That would put me over the hump for sure. I would be able to pay the full amount for my first year of tuition at the University of Rochester.

What was even better than that? My mom had agreed to let me borrow her car whenever I worked so that I didn't have to walk or bike ride to the Sunrise Mall. It was only a mile and a half, but definitely not fun in ninety-five-degree heat or when it was pouring rain. I was psyched.

My mom was really nice. I was so grateful for her. The car was a two-door silver Datsun 210 which was only 165 inches and less than two thousand lbs. Though it was two years old and not a sports car (my dream at that time), it was mine to drive. And I was so happy that I would have a car for the summer before college.

On this particular day, I had worked at Nathans from noon, getting a full nine hours in: almost $40. This would be enough for two full tanks of gas! Our manager had told us we were closing the store early because of the holiday.

Harold had mentioned his brother was having a party at his parent's house and I was definitely in. I didn't know him well, since he went to Massapequa High School and I went to Berner High School, but he was definitely cool.

He was the kitchen guy during the evenings. He had "seniority" because he had worked at Nathans since 1979. But he didn't have a car. And he knew I did. So, it was a win-win. I got to go to the party and he got a ride home.

He lived near the Bar Harbour shopping center and there seemed to be few cars on the road. It was almost 9:20 p.m. when he told me to take the shortcut to go local instead of that 'main street' off of Merrick Road. I made the left and then the right and was cruising down the street, when I heard the fireworks start. As I approached the cross street, another blast and lots of gun smoke exploded into the air. I sped up as I approached the intersection. I'm not sure why to this day. Instinct? Intuition?

The screech of metal hitting metal was frightening. We got out of my mom's car and immediately realized we were not on the road, but across the street in the front yard of the house on the corner. The wooden fence was in pieces.

Looking at the car itself, the front at least, was untouched. But then I looked at the left side of the car. The whole back of the car was smashed in. It was clear if I had not sped up, the other car would have gone right into my door and me. This was before airbags. It would not have been pretty for my perfectly fit and agile teenage body!

I was obviously in shock. I couldn't stand, so I just sat down on the curb and began sobbing. A crowd began to form and people came out of the house and asked if we were okay. I remember repeating, "I think so," multiple times.

After a few minutes of shock, I somehow remembered to give someone my parent's house number to call them (yes, this was before mobile phones existed).

As I wept, these thoughts started going through my head:

My summer is ruined! What would my parents do to me? How bad would the whipping be? How loud will the yelling be? Will they make me pay for the car damages? Will I be able to go to college, or will I have to use my savings for the damages? How much will that be?

87

As these thoughts were running through my head, my parents arrived. All I can remember is them giving me hugs. That made me weep even more. I guess that is when it hit me: I was lucky to be alive.

And believe it or not, I did not have even a scratch on me. Nor did Harold.

Yes, we were both extremely lucky.

After giving the policemen my statement, my parents had the car towed and drove me home. They didn't once reprimand me or scream at me. The whipping I endured was all in my mind, as I didn't sleep that night.

Sad, depressing, horrible thoughts kept running through my mind as I kept on criticizing myself. I reprimanded myself more than anyone else:

How could you have been so stupid? Why didn't you slow down? How could you have missed the stop sign? Why were you even going to that silly party? You don't even know Harold or his brother well? Why do you care what other people think? And on and on.

Yes, you are usually your own worst critic and it can indeed be damaging to your own progress and achieving your goals.

My parents were sympathetic to me throughout that summer knowing how much that car had meant to me. The car was totaled and insurance mostly paid for another car.

My parents let me use my savings to pay for the University of Rochester and I spent the summer walking or biking to Nathans. I actually felt grateful for my parents and my situation. There were at least a few times during the summer and the coming years when I realized that five miles per hour was probably the difference between me being alive and going to another realm.

And what other things was I grateful for? The car accident made me the most responsible seventeen-year-old-driver out there. I became a much slower, defensive driver. I was much more cognizant of my surroundings. I stopped at every stop sign—a full stop. It took many years of coaxing from my parents and friends to change this behavior.

What else was I grateful for?

I was just grateful for being alive.

I was grateful for my health.

I was grateful for being able to go to the University of Rochester after all.

I was grateful for my parents being rational and kind and supportive.

I was grateful for automobile insurance.

What can you be grateful for that you take for granted every day?

What does gratitude mean to you?

I tell my clients to write down five things they are grateful for every morning and every night. It doesn't have to be amazing items. It can just be that the sun is out or you experienced another day in the greatest city in the world (I am biased, but to me, Manhattan is!), or you enjoyed a great smoothie.

Whatever it is, it doesn't have to be huge. Just write it down. I do believe being grateful for Lauren and Morgan (something I write in my gratitude journal every day) is huge though. The miracle of life is something we take for granted, but for me it is a miracle that the exact mix of DNA became who you are. And, of course, from that tiny microscopic cell you became you. Now, that is a true miracle! Isn't it?

As Mike Dooley says in his *New York Times* best seller, *Infinite Possibilities: The Art of Living Your Dreams*: "Gratitude is powerful and it *does* work magic, so it's great to work it into your affirmations whenever you can. Give thanks and praise to life, its grace, and its unfailing principles for having *already* manifested your dreams, say things like 'Thanks for surrounding me with health, wealth, friends, and laughter! Thank you, thank you, thank you!,' and really feel it!"

Now, those are some powerful statements! Try it!

So, why is gratitude a part of my unconventional rules? Being grateful is important to becoming wealthy, because the more grateful you are, the more things come into your life for you to be grateful about. This is what is known as the Law of Attraction.

Consider starting a gratitude journal and writing what you are grateful for. Since you are focusing on the good in your life, there must be more good things that will come into your life.

And speaking of Mike Dooley, I wanted to share a story that is another example of the reason I am so grateful for Mike, his *New York Times* best seller, *Infinite Possibilities,* and the training program, Infinite Possibilities: The Art of Changing Your Life.

Many of you know that for most of my life my biggest fear was public speaking. So, read on to hear how I surmounted this anxiety in the speech, "Overcoming Fear." This is the speech I gave at Mike's Train the Trainer Course for Infinite Possibilities (IP) in New Orleans in March 2018, to a group of individuals being trained by Mike to teach IP:

"I was twelve years old. I was on the stage at Unqua Elementary School in Massapequa on Long Island, New York. It was my sixth-grade play, and when they came to me, instead of saying my lines, I just stood there—frozen! It seemed like thirty minutes to me. Thankfully, they finally skipped over me and no one else remembered those very, very long thirty seconds except me.

What's *your* biggest fear? Think about it. What are you really afraid of? Write it down!

Napoleon Hill, in my favorite book, *Think and Grow Rich*, enumerates six fears. Oops, I apologize, Mike. I mean my second-favorite book!

The six ghostly fears that Napoleon Hill lists are:

1. Fear of criticism

2. Fear of ill health

3. Fear of poverty

4. Fear of old age

5. Fear of the loss of love

6. Fear of death

Most people rank fear of death first. But I will tell you there is one fear that Napoleon completely misses: the fear of public speaking. After that play, whenever I had to stand up in front of a group of more than two people, I made sure to bring my notes just in case. If I froze, I used my note cards!

Fear of public speaking was my number one fear for sure. Death—nah! I had a feeling long ago that death meant a new beginning, not an end.

So, again, what is your biggest fear? And what baby steps can you take to overcome it?

Let me tell you my story.

In July 2016, I reached out to a woman I knew, who was a health coach. I had decided to shut down my hedge fund after three years because I had figured out my life's purpose. I know it sounds like a cliché, but I had figured out that I was supposed to teach others about financial literacy and how to become financially free. So, I made a huge decision in December 2015 to shut down my hedge fund and become a prosperity coach.

I then reached out to Kirsi to ask her how she got clients and to pick her brain as it were.

Why did I shut down my hedge fund?

Well, I went to a conference in December 2015, and they had a guest speaker talking about stocks and stock options. He spoke about Facebook (FB) and how you would have made five to ten times your money investing in FB in May of 2013, along with similar stories.

I felt sick to my stomach. See, you can lose money in options; they are not riskless. And more importantly, this man was being, at the very least, misleading, and at the worst, lying to these people.

I went home that night and couldn't sleep and realized that my true purpose in life was teaching others about financial literacy and helping them become financially free. I truly believed I could do a better job than the guest speaker did.

I went into my office the next morning and emailed my investors saying, "I am shutting down the fund. I figured out my true purpose in life is to help others become financially literate and move toward financial freedom."

I had no idea the conversation with Kirsi, though, would be a life-changing event in its own right.

I was talking to Kirsi in July 2016, asking her questions, and at the end of all my queries, she says to me, "So, will I see you in October?"

I said, "Why?"

And she said, "Because Playing the Matrix is coming to New York."

I said, "Playing the what?"

She exclaimed, "you must know *Notes from the Universe*. Don't you get the daily emails?"

I said "No, I actually don't get that."

She said, "Really—you don't know Mr. Universe, Mike Dooley?" So, I start racking my brain and I get a picture in my head of Arnold Schwarzenegger. But Kirsi explains to me about Mike and his *Notes from the Universe*.

I arrived at the Omega Institute in October 2016 not having done any research on Mike or Playing the Matrix. Kirsi is trustworthy. I took her recommendation and I went.

The first day, Mike tells his story about being an accountant and about the first chapter of *Infinite Possibilities* which is called "Thoughts Become Things." Chills ran through my body. And I ran up to him after that session and showed him my email signature from when I'd started my hedge fund in 2013. It said: "Thoughts are things." This was from my second-favorite book, *Think and Grow Rich*, the one that has sold more than one hundred million copies!

But let's talk about more synchronicities.

I discussed how I started my career as an actuary, and Mike discussed at Playing the Matrix how he started his career as an accountant.

Does anyone know the difference between an actuary and an accountant?

An actuary looks at his feet when he talks to you; an accountant looks at your feet.

And they say an accountant is an actuary with charisma.

I don't believe in coincidences, only synchronicities. Because, besides the actuary and accountant comparison, and the "thoughts are things" vs. "thoughts become things," we also had the book, *The Secret*, in common.

The Secret also changed my Life. How, you might ask?

The book talks about this feather that this man imagined in his head. And every morning when he awakened, he thought about this feather then thought about it again every night before he went to sleep. Then one day he was walking down the street and saw this feather that he had thought about in his mind: A thought had become a thing.

At this point, I recounted to Mike my story about cotton balls that I described in Chapter 6, Rule #4: What does Visualizing have to do with Money?

For years afterward, I had these cotton balls filled with dirt and sand on my desk. A thought had become a thing. And *The Secret* had changed my life too.

Clearly, Chapter 1 of *Infinite Possibilities* really resonates with me. But let me talk briefly about "acting as if" and baby steps.

After the Playing the Matrix conference at the Omega Institute in Rhinebeck, New York in October 2016, I realized I needed to take some baby steps to move myself forward toward my dream of helping at least one hundred thousand people become financially free. I was still working on shutting down my fund but Playing the Matrix is all about eliminating the cursed hows and thinking about end results. So I visualized and 'acted as if.'

At the end of the Playing the Matrix course, I jumped up on stage. And I had someone take a picture of me speaking. And … here I am today having visualized myself speaking in front of you eighteen months ago.

But what baby steps did I take?

First, I signed up for Toastmasters, like Mike did, and started giving speeches. Yes, really.

The guy who was so fearful he had to bring notes to every presentation he made throughout his career and have every slide written out, joined Toastmasters! And they said "don't use notes!" What?!

Well, I've now given over fifty speeches at Toastmasters. But, most importantly, I was able to give a seventeen-minute speech at my daughter Lauren's Bat Mitzvah in front of almost two hundred people on March 4th, 2017 without my index cards. In fact, in 2019, I gave another very important speech at Morgan's Bat Mitzvah in front of more than two hundred people for about fifteen minutes, also without any note cards.

And Mike mentioned talking at a rotary club when I attended Playing the Matrix. I thought that would be a great idea. I put it on my list of to-do items for when I got back home.

The evening of the last day of the Playing the Matrix conference after I had returned home, I received an email from the president of my local rotary club asking me to speak—yes, that same day!

Another time, one of my IP trainees asked me in 2017 if I wanted to give an introduction to IP at her Unitary Church. And who knew—I was good enough to be asked to come back and give another Introduction to *Infinite Possibilities* in January 2018 and 2019.

What other baby steps have I taken?

Besides joining Toastmasters, I organized a Meetup called Infinite Possibilities on meetup.com. Yes, amazingly enough, there wasn't one in Manhattan. I started one and now we have over one hundred and fifty members in the Meetup.

I also took another baby step after coming back from Mike's Train the Trainer conference in Santa Fe, New Mexico, in 2017. I reached out to three people who were mentioned as website designers; they could help build a website. Appio Hunter graciously offered to help me for a very small fee. He did more for less. He may be one of the most giving people I've met.

Now someone can sign up online on my website that he built (https://www.salaurmor.com/) for an introduction to Infinite Possibilities training or a full day training session. They can even sign up for the latest prosperity coaching workshop or for a thirty-minute free prosperity coaching session.

I have now trained almost twenty people in Infinite Possibilities, and I have given a free introduction to another hundred in the last two years.

I am so grateful for Kirsi for connecting me with Mike Dooley, and of course, all the people who call themselves IPPIEs.

You can do this.

You are the allower of the good that you long ago created. And it is high time that you allowed the good that you long time ago created to manifest into your life.

I believe in you!

Thank you!"

That was the speech I gave in March 2018 to over one hundred Infinite Possibilities trainees. I am so grateful for having had the opportunity to speak in front of so many loving, powerful manifestors including Mike and Andy Dooley. What a rush it was as many of the people laughed at my actuary jokes and came up to me afterward to tell me that they were inspired.

The most powerful part, though, was when I saw multiple people jump up on the stage at the break and take pictures in front of that podium in New Orleans like I had done in 2016 in Rhinebeck, New York. Yes, they were inspired to act as if! They wanted to speak in 2019 at the Train the Trainer conference in Denver, Colorado!

Now, I want to address a part of that speech that may be controversial. Some people say the book *The Secret* is absurd. They say you can't just sit at home all day and manifest your dreams and desires. And I totally agree that you can't just think your way to success. It doesn't work—solely—that way.

If I had just sat at home all day I would not have seen the cotton balls in Crawford Park. But more importantly, I'm pretty sure *The Secret* was not suggesting that to get rich you should sit at home and just meditate and do affirmations all day. In teaching Mike Dooley's *New York Times* best seller, *Infinite Possibilities: The Art of Living Your Dreams*, as a Certified Infinite Possibilities Trainer, we discuss "taking action," which is essentially Chapter 4:"Life is Waiting For You".

In teaching his material, I ask trainees, "Have you ever met a billionaire who just sat home all day and meditated and visualized their dreams and desires?" Of course not! You have to go out into the world and take action! In fact, Mike specifically says to "Supplement the more traditional, *physical actions* (emphasis added) you take as you move toward your dream ..."

I also tell the story to trainees about the guy who decided he was going to win the lottery. Every morning, he checked the newspaper. Every day, he waited by the phone for the call, and at the end of the day, he hadn't won. Day after day this would go on and he was getting more and more frustrated. One evening after checking the newspaper and waiting by the phone with no call, he went into his backyard and screamed at the heavens: "What is taking so long? What do I have to do?" After doing this for several evenings and getting angrier and louder, he finally got a response: "Meet me halfway! Buy a ticket!"

You see, you have to take action, even if you want to win the lottery.

This is a question I get from a lot of clients and audiences when I've talked about the three BIG secrets to having more money. B stands for Beliefs (Rule #1), I is for Intuition (Rule #2), and G is for Giving (Rule #6).

You've talked a lot about beliefs. So, why don't I just play the lottery every day and sit at home and believe with all my heart that I will win and then I will?

First of all, does playing the lottery give you a burning desire? I believe that not only do you have to have a belief, but also a burning desire for what you want. In addition, it would be really beneficial if you were doing something you are passionate about—something you love to do. When I was managing my hedge fund, the first six to twelve months were really blissful. I was so happy working on living my dream and doing what I had wanted to do for so many years (and getting paid for it!).

If you have a burning desire for winning the lottery, visualize yourself winning—and doing good with all the money, and your belief level is an eight, nine or ten, then go for it. But my guess is that for most of you, it is really hard to have a burning desire to win the lottery and given the probability of winning is so low, you are likely to have high doubt and thus, your belief level won't be an absolute knowing (a 10!) or close to it.

Another important reason comes from the best seller, *The Slight Edge*, by Jeff Olsen:

"Have you ever noticed that when you read stories about lottery winners, they are hardly ever bank presidents, successful entrepreneurs, or corporate executives? That they never seem to be people who were already financially successful before they bought that winning ticket? Have you ever wondered why? It's because successful people never win the lottery. You know why? Because they don't buy lottery tickets. Successful people have already grasped the truth that lottery players have not: success is not a random accident. Life is not a lottery."

Another interesting fact is that on average, a lottery winner's net worth five years after he or she wins the lottery is actually lower than the day before they won the lottery.

Why?

It is because their mindset is not primed for success. It is still poverty conscious. And, when that is true, their mindset rules, and eventually the physical reality of money in the material world drops back to where their mindset is—in poverty. And as Dan Lok says in *F.U. Money*: "Since lottery winners make their F.U. Money, the financial security is an illusion. They never acquire the F.U. Money mindset and skill sets they need to put their money to good use. Eventually, most lottery winners will blow all the money they win on nonsense and still go broke … Why does this happen? Because they relied on luck alone to get the money. Luck wasn't enough to carry them into the future and assure that they would stay rich. To do that, it takes intelligence."

That is why it is so much more fun to work on a business or investment idea that really gets you excited, gets you so happy that you are making a difference in the world that you would love doing it even if it didn't make you financially free. And that is when it absolutely will. Because you are in the moment, enjoying, happy, feeling bliss and joy and it's fun. That is what life is about anyway. Isn't it?

Now, some people say you have to take massive action. You have to work hard to be rich and successful. And, in fact, as I alluded to in my speech in New Orleans in March 2018, in 2009 I had changed my beliefs about working hard. And I stopped working more than seventy hours a week like I had in 2008. I began working more strategically and more productively. And a funny thing happened, I received a check in January 2010—my bonus check—that was multiples what I had ever made in my life. It was actually within one thousand dollars of a check I had put up on my ceiling above my bed the day after the cotton balls had manifested on May 31, 2008. What is immensely important to realize, of course, is that I took action! I didn't sit at home and stare at that check all day long, saying "I don't know how, I don't know why, but I do know this is coming." I only did that right when I woke up and right before I went to sleep. I didn't sit home all day in 2009 and meditate and visualize. That only took place for a few minutes in the morning and again at night.

Besides looking at that check on my ceiling every morning and every night, I went out into the world. I analyzed financial statements, went to conferences, talked to companies, modeled out their earnings, cash flow, and balance sheets, and I believed. I also had a burning desire for that money to come to me.

I'm pretty sure *The Secret* is not advising that you sit home all day and read the book over and over again. And then meditate and visualize and watch the movie, *The Secret*, repeatedly. What it does advise is for you to do that, plus get out into the world and *take action.*

That is a huge part most people when they discuss *The Secret* miss. And I believe it is also a big reason the book has been dismissed as a bunch of 'woo-woo' and 'psychobabble' that doesn't work.

The law of attraction is not only about like attracting like and thoughts becoming things, but it is about being so happy and grateful with your life that you want to go out and do the things you love because they are fun. And because you get to interact with other people who are fun, loving, and great souls who you can learn from and maybe even collaborate with. To me, that is what the law of attraction and *The Secret* are all about.

Go ahead and meditate and visualize! Get out into the world and take some action too. You'll want to, because it feels right, it's fun, and most importantly, it is what you want to do.

To complete the discussion, it is important to note that the importance of gratitude's impact on your happiness has been proven scientifically. Martin Seligman, the *New York Times* multi-best-selling author, recommends playing this game: "Every night for the next week, set aside ten minutes before you go to sleep. Write down three things that went well today and why they went well … The three things need not be earthshaking in importance … but they can be … Next to each positive event, answer the question 'Why did this happen?' … Writing about why the positive events in your life happened may seem awkward at first, but please stick with it for one week … The odds are that you will be less depressed, happier, and addicted to this exercise six months from now."

Seligman goes on to say that two of the exercises—what went well (described in the paragraph above and similar to my gratitude journal) and the signature strengths exercise (which refers to those character strengths that are most essential to who we are. They are strengths that usually [but not always] appear toward the top of one's profile of results after taking the free survey https://www.viacharacter.org/www/Character-Strengths-Survey)—"markedly lowered depression three months and six months later … and also substantially increased happiness through six months."

I will conclude this chapter with a powerful gratitude meditation by Andy Dooley. Listen to this daily and it will raise your vibe: https://soundcloud.com/vibrationactivation/sets/shower-of-good-vibes

Key Points from Chapter 7:

• Stop worrying. It is just "negative future planning." Why not think about what you do want to happen in the future, not what you don't?

• Write down five items you are grateful for every morning right when you wake up and five things every night just before you go to sleep. They don't have to be massive, crazy, miraculous things either. Sometimes I write down "I am grateful today is over!" You can write down you are grateful for just being alive, for a sunny day (or a snowy day if you like to catch snowflakes on your tongue while jogging outside like I do), for your home, for your car, for air conditioning or heating, for your health, your faith, your intuition, or for your family. What about being grateful for a mentor in your life, like a Mike Dooley? And the things you are grateful for don't have to be different every day.

• The more you focus on what you are grateful for already, the more things will come into your life that you will be able to find gratitude for.

CHAPTER

8

Rule #6: If I give my money away, I'll have less money—not more—how does that work?

How can giving (Rule #6) help you to become financially free? And why is it an unconventional money rule?

As Mike Dooley says in *Infinite Possibilities*, "Our brain—logic—tells us that the more we take out, the less we'll have, but that's because our brain is only accustomed to assessing physical reality. Its sense of logic doesn't work in the spiritual realm. In fact, the opposite is true with the universal bank account: the more we take out, the bigger the balance gets! If you go to your universal ATM for one hundred dollars, that's what it'll give to you; but if you go for one million, it'll be there too—with faith."

Mike himself is an amazingly giving human being. He tells the story of how after writing *Infinite Possibilities,* he wanted to teach the material to everyone he could get in touch with.

He reached out to various prisons in Florida where he was living. One eventually responded: The Orange County jail. Norberto Perez, who was in charge of the Addictions program agreed that Mike could come in and talk to some inmates. Of course, Mike was not getting paid to do this, but he developed a program that taught the key concepts of his best seller: thoughts become things, beliefs, emotions, taking action, etc. All of this on a pro-bono basis. Mike gave a tremendous amount of his valuable time to this endeavor. I tell people "Time is our most valuable resource."

All this giving came back to him multiple times in the years that followed. Jordan Peterson, in his enlightening book, *12 Rules For Life*, asks: "What should I do when greed consumes me? Remember that it is truly better to give than to receive. To give, is to do what you can to make things better. The good in people will respond to that, and support it, and imitate it, and multiply it, and return it, in a (manner) so that everything improves and moves forward."

"Your Attention, Please … Your Attention, Please … This … is the Universe. Today I'll be recording your every thought and emotion, no matter how 'good' or 'bad,' no matter how generous or stingy, and no matter how helpful or hurtful they may be. And everything I record … will be played back for you, as soon as possible, as some type of physical manifestation in time and space. Thank you, that is all, The Universe" — Mike Dooley, *Notes from the Universe*.

For me personally, I know when I give, I just feel better. It shows me that I have plenty to spare and share.

I found out how much better I felt when I was helping others. As I detailed in my best seller, *Mindful Money Management: Memoirs of a Hedge Fund Manager*, I started doing five nice things a day as recommended by Sandy Forster in *How to be Wildly Wealthy Fast*.

It can be a simple act like holding the elevator for someone in your building, holding the door open when you enter a room, or saying "bless you" when someone sneezes. I found it easy to be nicer to others and that truly helped my mindset.

As Napoleon Hill stated in *The Master Key to Riches*, "We have never yet found a truly happy person who was not engaged in some form of service by which others were benefited. And we do know many who are wealthy in material things, but have not found happiness."

As I did more for others, I found opportunities to help others increased. On the weekends I didn't have my daughters with me, I would go into Manhattan to work in 2013 through 2016 when I managed my hedge fund. Invariably,

I would see visitors from out of town using a map or searching their smartphone for their next destination.

This started happening so much I actually thought I should invest in a firm that gave out maps throughout Manhattan like they do in foreign cities like Split in Croatia. Anyway, I was giving assistance and feeling good about helping others that were lost in the concrete jungle I call home.

I also saw more and more people needing assistance with their luggage as they entered or exited the subway. They were surprised to have a native New Yorker asking if they needed help lugging a suitcase up several flights of stairs.

In April and May of 2014, I wrote a piece entitled "My Dream Job" for *The Actuary* magazine. The article was published in the June/July 2014 edition. I was surprised to see my article highlighted on the cover of the magazine!

I received a number of calls and emails from actuaries interested in learning more about my transition from working as a traditional actuary at New York Life to a hedge fund manager. Gladly, I met with a number of them and had very enriching telephone calls with others.

I explained to them how my belief and *knowing* that I would get to my current seat was what actually got me there. I did what Napoleon Hill stated in *Think and Grow Rich,* which was, "Whatever the mind of man can conceive, and bring himself to believe, he can achieve."

Tony Robbins talks about giving in his life-changing book, *Money: Master the Game.* "When giving outside of ourselves is done right, when it feels like a choice, when it connects us with others, and when it makes a clear impact, even small gifts can increase happiness, potentially stirring a domino effect of generosity."

Robbins also says this about giving: "It primes our brain; it trains and conditions us to know that there's more than enough. And when our brain believes it, we experience it."

I also began a giving program which was inspired by Paul Pompeo, a member of my Mastermind Group back in 2012.

I handed out the book *Think and Grow Rich* to strangers, acquaintances and friends. I also found time to help people changing jobs or looking for jobs. We met for coffee or a drink. And I squeezed in some time to go to the Food Bank For New York City's warehouse to see their operations.

These little acts felt right and helped me get through some trying times. I remembered Sandy Forster saying that your life is a dream for billions of people around the world. If they could just switch places with you, even for a day, it would be their dream come true.

In 2018, I found that giving to the numerous homeless people in Manhattan felt right. For example, I gave to a woman in her fifties who was rummaging through the garbage in Grand Central Station to find bottles and cans for the deposit money. I gave her enough money for hundreds of cans and bottles, and she was very grateful.

And strange enough, in the days and weeks that followed, the number of book sales and new clients that came to me multiplied. Coincidence? I don't believe in coincidences, only synchronicities!

In a Toastmasters speech in 2018 that won the Manhattan-area contest, I had this to say about giving:

> "No investor will ever talk about this, but it is probably the most powerful way to become financially free. Giving creates Karma. You reap what you sow! Sir. John Templeton, considered by some to be the world's greatest investor, said that he didn't know anyone who had given 10 percent of what he earned to charities over a ten-year period who didn't massively grow his financial wealth.
>
> Now, some of you may be thinking, *what*? If I give my money away, I will have *less* money. How does that work? Well, let me explain something. The reason is that money is energy—the more

you give, the more you open yourself up to receive. The more you put that energy out into the world by giving and sharing with others, the more that energy must come back to you.

The more you give, the more you create a belief in your ability to receive more.

By giving as little as 10 percent, you are creating the belief that you are abundant and worthy and there is more than enough to go around.

And giving doesn't have to be just money. You can give your time to those in need. You have a unique gift or talent—share it with the world.

You could give a smile or a compliment to a stranger, or give a speech at your Toastmasters club.

Only by giving are you are able to receive more than you already have.

I can tell you when I started a giving program to the Food Bank For New York City and started doing five nice things a day, I felt I had plenty to spare and share. I felt more abundant!

Giving can indeed change the world and I hope this speech does inspire someone to start."

Sir John has also said that "The secret of success is giving not getting. Those who are grown up, give. The immature do not. It is wise to practice giving in every area of life."

As Mike Dooley says, "By inviting … (the magic) into your thoughts with gratitude and giving thanks that what you want is already yours even though you don't physically see it yet, you prepare the way for unlimited withdrawals."

Aren't there limited amounts of money in world? How do I get my 'fair' share?

After discussing abundance and giving in many presentations, this is the often-asked question. And I answer that I truly believe there is an almost infinite amount of money on earth and more and more is created every day. In fact, if we redistributed the wealth of the earth (I'm not saying do this. I am not a socialist—I am just using this as an example), then all 7.5 billion people would have approximately $1,000,000. A lot larger number would be financially free than are now!

As Abraham Hicks said: "Do you ever hear anyone say, well, I've been so well for so many years, and there are so many people out there who are sick, and I've been using up all the wellness value for so long that I've decided that I'm going to be sick for a while to allow more sick people to be well. I'm doing this because I've been getting more than my fair share of wellness. You never say that because you don't see it as a pile of something that can be divvied out. You accept that as a vibrational relationship in some way.

Humans, say, well, that one was just unlucky in sickness and that other one was just lucky in wellness. But it's not like that at all.

There is a vibrational abundance that is being realized by some and denied by others. There's not a big pile of resources that you're divvying up. Somebody didn't set the monetary fiscal standard for the Universe. And that is all that is out there and now you have to steal it or trade it ... This is a vibrational reality that you're moving into."

In the groundbreaking novel, *The One Minute Millionaire*, Mark Victor Hansen and Robert G. Allen discuss giving as expanding money. They state that "Just like water exists in three forms—ice, liquid, and vapor—we find it useful to think that money exists in three dimensions: the frozen state (material), the liquid state (mental), and the ethereal or spiritual state. When you give money from an attitude of gratitude and abundance, it thrusts you from the material state into the ethereal or spiritual dimension."

They go on to say that "Just like water expands when its heated, money expands when it is given away. Giving literally magnifies, multiplies, and exponentializes money."

They conclude by saying that "The Enlightened Millionaire knows that giving money actually expands in the spiritual dimension (100 percent × 10 percent = 1,000 percent (actually, being a math major, this is not an accurate calculation; I think what they meant was 100 percent × 10 = 1,000 percent)). This is spiritual math. Tithing is a money multiplier, not a money subtractor."

"Giving demonstrates a belief that you are provided for. It's an act of faith that implies you will remain whole, that what you gave will come back to you, and that love is what matters most. And when you believe these things they'll become your reality, and abundance will be showered upon you as if the heavens had opened up," — Mike Dooley, *Notes from the Universe*.

Get ready for massive abundance. It is on the way!

Key Points from Chapter 8:

- Giving done in a state of appreciation for all that you have will physically send out signals that literally make you feel better.

- As Mark Victor Hansen and Robert G. Allen stated, giving money actually causes expansion in the spiritual dimension.

- Giving doesn't only have to be about money. You have a special talent or gift! Why not share that with the world. You could simply give a smile or a compliment to a stranger.

- Give to those in need.

- As Tony Robbins said, giving "primes our brain; it trains and conditions us to know that there's more than enough." And when our brain believes it, we experience it.

This part of the book goes into the processes, the procedures, and the action steps to having more money. Hopefully the first part of the book inspired you. You know what you want. You already asked for lots of things in this lifetime. You want to take some action because you are inspired. It feels right. It is a knowing. And you know it is going to be fun. It is going to be joyous and you are going to have a good time doing the action steps. You want to take some action. Read ahead and whatever resonates, take action on, and whatever doesn't, ignore.

PART

2

The Processes

1

Rule #7: Where is my Cash Going?

"You want me to keep track of *everything* I spend for the next thirty days? Are you kidding me? I don't have the time to do that!"

Do you have the time to post on Facebook, Instagram and Snapchat every day?

Do you have time to watch sports this weekend or play golf with your buddies?

Do you have time to watch that movie or your favorite TV program?"

If you answered yes to any of those questions and you are not budgeting, you do have the time. You are just not making it a priority! I know people will spend a hundred and fifty hours of planning for one year for a five-hour event—their wedding. Yet, they won't spend fifty hours a year (one hour a week) for financial freedom planning. Isn't thirty years of your life (or more) worth fifty hours a year??

"Okay, Okay. I get it. What do you want me to do?"

This is a conversation I had with one of my clients. In fact, she had done really well. We had started with just keeping track of expenses for three days and then graduated to five days and then a week. But when we went from one week to four, it became too much.

Why?

Isn't your financial freedom worth thirty to sixty minutes a week?

But what is a budget? This is Rule #7!

Here are the steps:

1. Keep track of every amount you spend for one day. Everything—yes. If you bought that pack of gum, write it down. If you purchased a coffee or a water or a diet soda, write it down. Maybe you love having that piece of chocolate or M&Ms (peanut or plain?); write that down. Write them all down.

2. I will give you a spreadsheet to put the amounts in (go to https://www.salaurmor.com/ and email me for your free spreadsheet for budgeting). There will be different categories including food, shelter, chocolate, massages, manicure/pedicure, lottery, fantasy games (baseball, football, etc.), gas, etc., etc.

3. You will put the amounts in the appropriate cell in the spreadsheet.

4. You will fill in your monthly income. This should be your net income after taxes and other automatic contributions for retirement savings like 401(k), 403(b), etc.

5. You will subtract #3 from #4 above to get your monthly net cash flow.

6. Is the total from step 5 positive? Congratulations. You are one of the single-digit percentage of adults who are not spending all they make. Is the result from step 5 negative? If yes, we have some work to do!

The next step is to determine how close or far away you are from financial freedom.

"Financial freedom is being able to spend time (as much as you want) with the ones you love." — Doug Nelson

What is your financial freedom number? Do you know? Let's calculate it.

It is the amount of passive income investments you have that generate enough income to cover your current or dream expenses so that you don't have to work if you don't want to.

For example, suppose your monthly expenses are $5,000. Then your annual expenses would be $60,000. To cover these expenses, you would need $1,000,000 earning a conservative 6 percent after tax ($1,000,000 × 6 percent = $60,000) to be financially free.

What is your current amount of passive income investments? These are investments that are outside of your retirement accounts that generate income without you having to work for them. If you have your own coaching business and you charge $500 per hour, all the hours you work do not count as passive income. That is active income!

Let's start with your net worth and then move to passive income.

What is your current net worth? Don't know?

Your net worth is your assets less any amounts you owe.

Let's start with your assets. Add up all your investments: stocks, bonds, mutual funds, exchange-traded funds (ETFs), your house, any vacation homes, rental real estate property, 401(k), 403(b), 457, annuities, Roth IRAs, traditional IRAs, cash value life insurance, and cash and short-term investments: checking, savings, money market, and CD accounts.

This is the amount of your total assets.

Now add up all your debt. This includes home equity loans, mortgage loans, credit card debt (only the amount that you don't pay off monthly), student loans, car loans, and payday loans, which I know some of you have.

Taking your total assets less your total debt is your net worth.

Subtract from your total assets any money you have in any retirement funds—those 401(k), 403(b), 457, Roth IRAs, traditional IRAs, and fixed and variable annuities. Also, your house, your cash-value life insurance, and cash and short-term investments earnings less than 2 percent (we could include them, but if this amount is less than $50,000, then the total annual income is less than $1,000). What is left over is the amount of your passive income investments.

You can see how close you are to financial freedom by subtracting your passive income investments from your financial freedom number. Remember, you calculated it above by multiplying your monthly expenses by 12 and then dividing by 6 percent). If it is less than $100,000, that is great. You are really close to financial freedom. If it is negative, then that means you are financially free already!

Congratulations!

I recommend that if you truly want to become financially free that you write down your dream expenses. That is the amount of expenses you would have if you were living your dream life.

First of all, this will help you get very specific about how you would live if you could live your dream life. The more specific the better. Instead of writing down that you would like to have a dream car worth at least $50,000, write down that you would like to own a blue convertible Maserati Quattroporte S with brown leather seats and a 424 HP V6 with intelligent RWD and semi-autonomous driving capabilities.

Why?

Because the more specific you can be with your dreams and desires, the more the subconscious mind will dwell on it, imagine it, and feel the feelings of driving it, with the top down and the wind blowing your hair (well if you have more hair than I do!).

Also, importantly to reach your goals, it is helpful if you know what your specific goals are. And once you write down all your dream material items, you can add up the costs of buying them outright or leasing them (you know my preference) and see what the amount your financial freedom number would then be.

Now, some people have asked me, "If I do this calculation, the passive income investments don't include all my investments in retirement vehicles like my 401(k)[2] or Roth IRA[3] (Individual Retirement Account)? What about them?"

Well, my flip answer is they don't count. But let me be more specific. They are all retirement vehicles which help you to save for age sixty-five or seventy, or later. If you want to retire earlier, then the goal is to create passive income vehicles that generate money *today and in the future*. The whole financial services industry was built around you giving them your money to invest for you and them charging you 0.5 percent, 1 percent, or more. This is not DIY investing (see Part 2, Chapter 5). But to be fair, you can also self-direct your investments in a Roth IRA or traditional IRA so that you can invest in real estate or individual stocks. If you have specific questions on these vehicles or how to self-direct, email me at Joel@SaLaurMor.com.

Here is another method that I highly recommend using. It will allow your cash flow to improve fast. The main points of the method are from one of my favorite books, *Ask and It is Given*, by Esther and Jerry Hicks (https://www.salaurmor.com/inspiration/#books)

---

2. Many employers offer a 401(k) plan to employees as part of their benefits package. The plan provides a tax deduction for both employer and employee when the employee puts money into their 401(k) account. While the main idea is that you put money into the plan pre-tax, it helps to understand how these contributions work. Normally, when you earn money as an employee, you have income taxes withheld on the money you earn. A 401(k) plan allows you to avoid paying income taxes in the current year on the amount of money you put into the plan. The amount you put in is not taxed, so you 'defer' your tax payment until later. The money grows tax deferred inside the plan. Tax deferred means that while the investments earn investment income, you do not pay tax on the investment gains each year. Instead, in retirement, you pay tax only on the amounts you withdraw at that time. You'll pay a 10 percent penalty tax *and* income taxes if you withdraw funds too early (before age 55 or 59 ½, depending on your retirement age).
3. A Roth IRA is a special retirement account that you fund with post-tax income (you can't deduct your contributions on your income taxes). Once you have done this, all future withdrawals that follow Roth IRA regulations are tax-free. There is no up-front tax deduction for Roth IRA contributions as there is with a traditional IRA; on the other hand, Roth distributions are tax-free. And because every penny you stash in a Roth IRA is your money, you can tap your contributions (but not your earnings on those contributions) at any time, tax-free and penalty-free.

- To begin the process, open up a spreadsheet. Start with the far left column, write a heading that describes your largest expense (it is usually your rent or your mortgage payment), and on the next line under the header, write the dollar amount. Circle this amount, which is the sum you are obligated to pay each month. On the third line, write the total amount of the debt outstanding

- Do the same for the second largest expense and the third, until you get to the smallest one.

- Across the top of all the columns write: "It is my desire to keep my promise regarding all these financial obligations, and in some cases, I will even do twice as much as required."

- Each time you receive a bill, get out your spreadsheet and adjust, if necessary, the minimum monthly amount that is required.

- The first time you receive a bill or when it's time to make the payment for the category on the far-right column of your spreadsheet (the smallest expense you have), write the check for exactly twice the amount that is required.

- Then, also write in the new amount of that outstanding balance.

- This may seem a little strange, but even if you don't have enough money to pay everything you owe in all the columns, be sure to double the payment in the far-right column.

- Now feel glad that you have kept your new promise to yourself to do your best to pay everything you owe, and to pay twice that amount in some cases.

- You are looking at your finances in a new way: creating a new vibration!

- If you will take the time to really enter everything you owe in the spreadsheet, your newly focused attention will begin to positively activate circumstances around the subject of money for you.

- Instead of feeling discouraged about getting bills in the mailbox, you will feel an eagerness to enter the bill in your spreadsheet.

- This will now shift your attitude, vibration, and things will begin to change in your financial picture. Money that you were not expecting will appear in your experience. Bargains will appear; your dollars will start going farther.

- Be consciously aware that these things are happening in response to your newly focused attention and the resultant shift in your vibration.

- As extra money appears, you will find yourself eager to apply another payment to the spreadsheet, and soon that debt *will* be repaid and you can eliminate that column from your spreadsheet.

Column after column will disappear as your financial gap between what is coming in and what is going out widens. Your sense of financial well-being will also improve as you play. And if you will take the game seriously, your vibration around money will shift so significantly that you can be debt-free in a very short period of time!

This experience is solidly supported by the following outlook:

"When the burden has lifted, when you feel lighter and freer, your resistance has lifted, and you are now in the position to allow the well-being to follow abundantly into your experience. People who have managed to find vibrational harmony with abundance—so that it is flowing to them and through them—are not depriving anyone else of that abundance. You cannot get poor enough to help the impoverished people thrive. It is only in your thriving that you have anything to offer anyone. If you want to be of help to others, be as tuned in as you possibly can. Money is not the root of all happiness nor the root of evil either. Money is the result of how somebody lines up energy. If you do not want money, do not attract it. But your criticism of others who have money holds you in a place where everything you do want, such as wellness, clarity, and well-being, cannot come to you either!" — *Ask and It is Given,* by Esther and Jerry Hicks

Let me be clear about my view on budgeting. Many have said budgeting is just focusing on lack, scarcity, and a poverty consciousness. To me, you need to know where you are, before you can figure out where you want to go. If you don't know how much money you are spending now—what your current expenses are—how can you figure out what it will take to become financially free, based either on current or dream expenses?

Yes, some financial "gurus" will tell you to cut out those lattes at Starbucks and drive only used cars (not a terrible idea actually), but that won't, in my humble opinion, get you to financial freedom. If you can't increase your income and especially generate passive income to exceed your expenses, you won't ever become financially free.

One important question people ask when I discuss financial freedom is:

Why does my money in retirement accounts (like a 401[k] or a traditional and ROTH IRA) not count toward my financial freedom number? I'm closer to financial freedom when I contribute to a retirement account, aren't I?

Here is the reason retirement accounts are not counted: If you are over 59.5, you have access to this money and can count it in your financial freedom number, but only if it is generating income for you through interest or dividends. Then, it is generating income for you now.

However, that is only true for a Roth IRA which you have already paid income taxes on. If you want to add in the money from a traditional IRA or 401(k) or 403(b), you should "tax affect" it by applying your tax rate (use 30 percent to be conservative) to the amount in it. For example, you have $100,000 in your 401(k) and you are over 59.5, then only $70,000 is available to you after taxes. Another important point is that you may not be generating *any* passive income if the account it is in does not pay dividends or is losing money (see Part 2, Chapter 3 for why you should DIY).

For those of you who can't get access to this money without paying a 10 percent penalty on top of the tax rate, it is not included in your passive income because it is not generating any income for you *now*. If you want to retire early—before 65 (some of you want to retire a lot younger than 65), then excluding your retirement savings is appropriate since it is not going to generate any income for you until much later in life. If you are 25, 35, or 45, you must wait at least 15 years to get access to your retirement money without a penalty. That is why I recommend excluding your retirement funds in the financial freedom calculations. If you have further questions, email me at Joel@SaLaurMor.com.

Key Points from Part 2, Chapter 1:

- Add up all your assets!

- Add up all your liabilities—all your debt.

- Calculate your net worth as your total assets less your total debt.

- Ask yourself: are your total assets growing or shrinking?

- Is your net worth going up or down each year? You should be calculating it at the beginning of January of each year for the prior year.

- What is your net cash flow? Is it positive or negative? This will give you a strong indication if you are moving closer to financial freedom or not.

- How much passive income do you have?

- What is your financial freedom number? How close are you to being financially free (hint: subtract from your financial freedom number your passive income investments)?

- How much credit are you using to support your lifestyle? The more credit outstanding, the more likely that you are farther from financial freedom (but read on to better understand credit in Part 2, Chapter 2) There are many good uses of credit, and if you can earn substantially more than what you are paying in credit, it probably makes sense to borrow.

2

Should I Use Credit?

"Of all the beings that have existence only in the minds of men, nothing is more fantastical and nice than Credit. It is never to be force; it hangs up on opinion; it depends upon our passions of hope and fear; it comes many times unsought-for and often goes away without reason; and, once lost, it is hardly to be quite recovered." — Charles Davenant, 1696

"You have to put more money into the account!"

"What are you talking about??"

"You hit your first loss on Friday! Didn't you notice? Aren't you tracking your daily performance?"

"Well, yes, but I was out of the office on Friday and I'm just getting in right now."

"Okay, well, let me know what you want to do. We can just shut it down here if you like!"

This was a conversation I had with the Chief Financial Officer (CFO) of the separately managed account I was managing in mid-2016. Readers of *Mindful Money Management* may remember the following passage when I was debating whether to open up the account:

"… we'd had numerous inquiries about setting up a 'first loss,' separately managed account into which I personally would put up my own money (as the first loss) and the investor would put an additional investment equal to ten times my own investment. This would allow us to increase both assets under management, and our profitability. It was something I was reluctant to do because of my lessons learned from the financial crisis about leverage. But I realized that if we didn't do something in the next year or so, the fund was unlikely to survive … At the time, my intuition, aka my sixth sense, was screaming NO! Was it fear or a sense of 'knowing'? At the time, I was not sure, but going with my intuition would have meant not even considering this extreme step …"

Now, you know the complete truth. My intuition was actually quite accurate. The call I received was because I was down more than 5 percent—which implied my money had declined more than 50 percent and I was required to put in more money. I initially did put in more money, but I couldn't sleep that night, and after having another poor day on the following Monday—losing more than 1 percent (10 percent more for me)—I remembered my initial intuitive hit not to do this. I called up the next day and apologized, saying I wasn't putting more money into the separately managed account.

As Kyle Bass stated in Tony Robbins' enlightening book, *Money: Master the Game*, "It's really how you deal with failure that defines you as a person."

As I discussed in *Mindful Money Management*, I clearly made this decision to please others. It was beneficial for my colleagues who were being underpaid and overworked. But if I was truly selfish and only thought about myself in 2015, I would not have invested more of my own savings to get additional outside money, thereby creating even more leverage.

So, is credit good or bad?

Well, it depends. What are you using it for?

In this particular case, credit was bad. It lost me a lot of money. But is using credit *always* bad?

Imagine you want to start a prosperity coaching business. You want to help thousands or hundreds of thousands of people become financially free. It is a "devout" business. But capital is needed. You have to market your coaching business over social media like Facebook, LinkedIn, Instagram, SnapChat, Pinterest, etc.

You also want to market off-line to various financial services companies, insurance agencies, and bank branches across the United States of America— to start. And then expand into other companies to teach their employees the basics of personal finance, manifesting, and investing.

Calculate your monthly fees for your online vendors like GoDaddy, Blue-Host, WordPress, Acuity Calendar, Quickbooks, Network Solutions, etc. Then you put together a business plan with expected coaching clients, book sales, seminars, webinars, YouTube advertising earnings, and "evergreen" products online.

You find a new bank that just got their first deposit from a local online and off-line marketer for $500,000.

You go to this bank. Meeting with your local small business lender there, you show him your annual expenses for year one: $650,000, but tell them you would like $500,000 to get started by hiring the marketer and incurring the related marketing expenses enumerated above. You explain to your lender how many people you are going to help, saying, "Just imagine if they became financially free and started using your bank for their businesses."

Your lender loves your ideas. He sees how you can leverage this coaching business from just a few individual clients to more than twenty individual coaching clients, while also consulting for companies and nonprofit orga-nizations. He sees that you could have a mastermind group on Facebook as well as teach other coaches to educate another one hundred fifty clients annually about investments, money mindset, manifesting, financial freedom, and budgeting and savings. And further, how you could teach and impact another twenty thousand people per year from seminars, webinars, and your online courses.

So, he lends you the $500,000. You then hire the marketer and pay him the $500,000. The marketer in turn deposits his newfound fortune at his local bank (your local small business lender).

How much money does the marketer now have in his bank account? He has $1,000,000. But how much money is actually in the bank? Just $500,000, since the bank took the initial deposit from the marketer and gave it to you. So ... how could this be? Well, this is called credit or leverage! The reason this happens is the service that you, as a prosperity coach, provide, is the collateral for the other $500,000.

Suppose the marketer does really well the next six months and he deposits another $500,000 into his account. He now has $1,500,000 sitting in his account. The bank has $1,000,000.

Imagine you go back to your friendly neighborhood banker. You ask him: "Actually, my marketing expenses are running quite high this first year, could I borrow another $500,000?" He agrees, knowing that this business is definitely going to pay him back easily, given the business plan in years two through six.

Now, the bank lends you another $500,000 and you give the money to the marketer who deposits another $500,000 into the account. The marketer now has $2,000,000 in his account. The bank has the same $1,000,000. Now, the leverage or credit is two times. And of course, this can go on many more times.

Credit is obviously based on trust. As the picture at Moody's Investors Service in downtown Manhattan states below: "Credit is based on "Man's Confidence in Man." Commercial credit is the creation of modern times and belongs in its highest perfection only to the most enlightened and best-governed nations. Credit is the vital air of the system of modern commerce. It has done more, a thousand times more, to enrich nations than all the mines of the world." — quoted from a speech by Daniel Webster in the Senate in Washington D.C., March 18, 1834.

So, again, is credit good or bad?

It depends.

It hinges on what you use the money for that you borrow. In the above example, I was using the money to acquire new clients and help individuals become financially literate and financially free. Assuming it worked, and I acquired new clients and generated $2,000,000 of revenues, would the $1,000,000 amount I borrowed have made sense?

Well, it is a trick question. Why?

Because you don't know how much of a return I made on the $2,000,000 and how much the bank required me to pay in interest. But if we assume that my margin on the $2,000,000 is 60 percent, and the interest rate on the $1,000,000 is 10 percent, then the $1,000,000 cost me $100,000 (assuming I paid back the loan in one year). And the return I received on the $1,000,000 was $1,200,000 (the $2,000,000 in revenues multiplied by my profit margin of 60 percent). Using credit and paying $1,100,000 to get earnings of $1,200,000 makes sense, right? Right!

Well, what if I had borrowed the $1,000,000 and the bank had charged 20 percent interest, and I had *only* acquired $1,000,000 of revenues. Well, assuming the same profit margin, my earnings would have been just $600,000. But in this case, I would have to pay the bank back $1,200,000 ($1,000,000 plus the 20 percent interest on the $1,000,000, or another $200,000).

In this case, it would not be a good use of credit. This simple example assumes that there is no further benefit from the credit utilized and the clients are for only one year. Of course, if I were able to retain all the clients and revenues for another year, then it *would* make sense, because the next year I would earn another $600,000 and have no debt outstanding).

Another use of credit is in your stock account. I know some sophisticated investors who took advantage of some very inexpensive stock prices in 2009. In most securities accounts, you can borrow from the brokerage company. You do have to fill out a form to establish a "margin account," which is just a fancy term for an account which is on credit. Anyway, these investors borrowed from their brokerage account at 5–10 percent interest rates, and invested in securities that proceeded to go up 50–100 percent over the next year or two. What a great use of credit!

According to David Graeber, in his International best seller, *Debt: The First 5,000 Years*, Calvin, alive in the 1500s, was one of the first to argue that charging interest on a loan was reasonable. "And by 1650 almost all Protestant denominations had come to agree with his position that a 'reasonable' rate of interest (usually 5 percent) was not sinful ... How was all this justified? ... first, Protestant thinkers all continued to make the old medieval argument about interesse: that 'interest' is really compensation for the money that the lender would have made had he been able to place his money in some more profitable investment." Graeber went on to explain that loans were 'legalized' in 1545, and being a lender became a real job—first to serve widows—who didn't have any other income source.

Let's talk more about the psychology of credit (aka debt). As David Graeber explained in his groundbreaking book, *Debt: The First 5,000 Years*: "Debt can be a way of punishing winners who weren't supposed to win. The most spectacular example of this is the history of the Republic of Haiti—the first poor country to be placed in permanent debt peonage. Haiti was a nation founded by former plantation slaves who had the temerity not only to rise up in rebellion ... but to defeat Napoleon's armies sent to return them to bondage. France immediately insisted that the new republic owed it 150 million francs in damages for the expropriated plantations ... The sum was intentionally impossible (equivalent to about $23 billion in 2018), and the resultant embargo ensured that the name, 'Haiti' has been a synonym for debt, poverty, and human misery ever since."

If one looks at the history of debt, there is a lot of confusion as to the morality of borrowing. In fact, Graeber explains that, in general, we humans believe two things about it: "(1) Paying back money one has borrowed is a simple matter of morality, and (2) Anyone in the habit of lending money is evil." So, how to do we borrow, if its evil to lend?

Have you bought a house?

Then you borrowed money—unless you paid for it all in cash!.

Graeber goes on to state that: "It is almost impossible to find a single sympathetic representation of a moneylender ... by definition one who charges interest." He goes on to explain that "The very word, 'usurer,' evokes images of loan sharks, blood money, pounds of flesh, the selling of souls, and behind them all, the Devil, often represented as himself a kind of usurer, an evil accountant (not an actuary!) ... biding his time until he can repossess the soul of a villain who, by his very occupation, has clearly made a compact with Hell."

How do you feel about borrowing money?

Have you borrowed from a bank?

A credit card company?

Your mom or dad? A sibling?

How does it make you feel? I recommend writing it down. Some people have told me they don't borrow. Why? Because they view it as "inappropriate." They bought their house for cash. The majority of us can't do that and won't!

This is not a book about cryptocurrencies, but it's important to note that "there's nothing new about virtual money ... this was the original form of money. Credit systems, tabs, even expense accounts, all existed long before cash ... First comes barter, then money, credit only develops later," according to Graeber.

How can money be defined? In my speech that you read in Chapter 8 from the Toastmasters Manhattan-area contest, I discussed how money is just energy.

Well, money is also a yardstick, as Graeber defines it. And he further explains that it is a yardstick that measures only one thing: debt.

He explains that any type of money from dollar bills to euros to coins are just IOUs. Essentially, "Banknotes are simply the promise to pay something of the same value as an ounce of gold. But that's all money ever is." So, a coin—whether it is gold or silver—is just a promise to pay something of the same value as that coin. As Graeber points out, the coin is not useful by itself. It's only useful if someone else will accept it. And we are back to Daniel Webster's quote that credit (aka debt) is just a measure of man's confidence or trust in another human being.

Look at a coin from your pocket. One side is heads—the symbol of the political authority which minted the coin—on the other side, the amount the coin is worth. One side reminds us that money is originally a relationship between people. The other shows "the coin as a thing, capable of entering into definite relations with other things," according to Graeber.

To conclude on the background on what money is, we must note that Graeber dates the use of paper money back to the issuance of municipal bonds, by the Venetian government in the twelfth century when the government needed some quick money because of wars. It required its citizens to provide it with a loan and promised to pay them 5 percent annual interest. However, David notes that "Only with the creation of the Bank of England in 1694 ... can (one) speak of genuine paper money, since its banknotes were in no sense bonds."

Some clients come to me asking how they can improve their credit score. Just to be clear, a credit score (also known as your FICO score after the reporting agency, **Fair Isaac Co**rporation) is used as a measure of your ability to borrow money. It also determines the interest rate at which you can borrow.

How is your FICO score calculated?

Well, it's a secret. No, that's not a joke. We don't know exactly how it is calculated, but we do know, based on the information that is asked, what items are important.

These are the five most important factors in your credit score:

1. Your payment history. What does this mean? It is just shorthand for your timeliness of past credit payments. This accounts for 35 percent of

your total FICO score, and is the largest proportion of the overall score. The more late payments you have on your credit report, the lower your score will be. The goal is to pay on time as much as possible.

2. Outstanding debt. What is this? It is the amount you already owe on your credit card bills, mortgage or student loans. Obviously the lower the amount the better, but ratios are important too (See below). This accounts for 30 percent of your FICO score.

3. Length of credit history. This represents 15 percent. So, if you are twenty-one, you are clearly going to have a much shorter credit history than someone who is my age. The longer the history the better.

4. Accounts in use (also known as your "credit mix"). The more accounts you have in use, the worse your credit score, in general. The presence of many accounts will negatively impact your score whether you are using them or not! It also depends on what types of accounts are outstanding. If you have a home equity loan outstanding, this is viewed more favorably because there is collateral behind it—your home! If you have a revolving credit line, this is effectively a line of credit. The lender, normally a bank, provides access to funds that the borrower can use at their discretion. It's a flexible, open-ended loan. A non-revolving line of credit is rated better because a credit limit is established, funds can be used for a variety of purposes, interest is charged as usual, but the pool of credit does not replenish after payments are made. Once you pay off the line of credit in full, the account is closed and can't be used again. Your credit mix accounts for 10 percent of the total FICO credit score.

5. Inquiries and new accounts. If you open multiple new accounts in a short period of time, this will negatively impact your credit score. Whenever a third party asks for your credit report (an "inquiry") this is recorded and if there are many inquiries in a short period of time, this will also negatively impact your score. Inquiries and new accounts make up 10 percent of your score.

How many credit cards do you have?

And can you benefit from credit?

First of all, I have been an investor in Discover Financial Services (DFS), the company that owns Discover Card, on and off since I was working at Citigroup since 2010.

As an investor, do I care if you have ten cards or one? Well, I do, because I want you to use your Discover card as much as possible. This is because DFS earns a fee--a transaction fee--every time you use the card.

Do I care if you pay your bill on time or not? I don't, as long as you pay your bill at some point. See, if you pay your bill late, you incur late fees and interest expenses, so DFS—and I, as a shareholder—make more money = more income.

Do I care if you don't pay your bill? Yes! If you don't ever pay your bill, the company doesn't get any money from you, nor do I. This is called a "charge-off." And if you never pay your bill, then DFS doesn't ever get paid—that is not good.

You should apply for more credit than you need so that you have capacity. For example, if you expect to be charging $1,000 a month, I would recommend asking for a credit limit of at least $3,000. This allows for unexpected items—say, a vacation or holiday presents. It also helps your credit score because of credit usage (see below).

Remember, the FICO score is also based on availability of credit compared to net income.

How can you improve your credit score?

One way is to reduce your amount of credit outstanding. The quicker and sooner you can pay off any credit cards the better. I worked with one client who had more than $20,000 in credit card debt outstanding and was paying over $1,000 a month. Though that seems like a lot of money, he actually wasn't paying down his balances. Thus, we opened a new account to transfer the balances onto a 0 percent interest rate card that was good for two years. This allowed him to come up with the cash in two years instead of right away, while not paying the average 11 percent interest rate which was causing the $1,000 a month.

Consider whether it makes sense to close a credit card account when you pay it off. It might seem logical to just close it, but this impacts your use of credit. For example, say you had five credit cards each with a $10,000 credit limit and you were using four cards for an average of $2,500 a month, or $10,000 in total. Your utilization rate would be $10,0000/$50,000 or 20 percent, but suppose you shut down the fifth card. Though the average amount was $2,500, you had only used this card for $500. Thus, the other cards had a total of $9,500. Now the utilization rate just jumped to $9,500/$40,000, or 24 percent. This would negatively impact your credit score.

Consider simply leaving the credit card that you just paid off outstanding, and now your utilization rate actually went down to 19 percent ($9,500/$50,000) from 20 percent ($10,000/$50,000).

How much of your credit limit you use will significantly impact your credit score. In the above example, you were using 20 percent of your credit limits. This is a small percentage and will positively impact your credit score. Going to 40 or 50 percent of your allowable credit limit will weaken your FICO score, and if it is much higher than that, the score will be very depressed.

You can improve your credit score by paying on time. If you have five cards, over twelve months, you have sixty payments. Being on time for just two years in a row will greatly improve your credit score. Setting up an automatic deduction out of your checking or money market account will ensure that the balance is paid each month. I recommend to my clients that they put their payments on auto-pilot this way.

Another way to improve your FICO score is to not apply for a new credit card—either from home or in the store—every time you get an offer. The more cards you apply for—especially within a three-month period—the lower your credit score will be. This is because each new credit card company does an inquiry as part of their background check, by looking at your credit report.

As I mentioned earlier, having multiple types of credit accounts will help your score. For example, having a student loan, mortgage loan, and a credit card is better for your score than having just three credit cards—even if the amounts of the loans are the same or similar.

Finally, if you are ever rejected for any type of loan, you get an explanation why. They should give you a specific explanation. For example, "you don't have a long enough credit history," or "you don't earn enough money," or "you are self-employed." Creditors prefer lenders whose compensation is consistent rather than volatile, like most entrepreneurs.

Some newly divorced women have asked me if they have a credit score since they were married to their husbands for twenty-five years. The answer is yes. They do have their own credit score and credit history *if* they had their own credit card or they had a joint credit card. This is also true if both names are on the title to the home mortgage. Importantly, you should know that whenever you share a card or co-sign a loan, that both of you are liable for the debt (this is also true if you have a credit card with a child).

Just know if you do not have a credit card in your own name or if you do not have joint cards, you will have trouble getting credit if you do get divorced or your spouse passes away.

One final comment on credit scores and credit usage.

Are you self-employed, an entrepreneur? If you are, then your income likely varies widely from month to month and year to year.

The credit card companies don't love entrepreneurs because they like consistency. They don't like income that varies—even if it is growing significantly from year to year. Personally, my income has ranged from less than $60,000 to more than seven figures in the last ten years. Credit card companies don't like that, despite my earnings potential being much, much higher than any employee could take home. They still prefer someone at a "steady" job even if that person is earning $50,000 a year, year in and year out. If that's you, then know that your credit score is starting out at a higher level than someone who is an entrepreneur.

You can get your credit score for free if you are a Discover cardholder. And, for full disclosure, if you own a Mastercard or American Express card, you can also ask for your credit score. They give it to you every month. If you are not a Discover cardholder, you can get a free credit report annually from www.annualcreditreport.com. You can obtain your credit score as well as your report at www.myfico.com. Remember, FICO stands for **Fair Isaac COrporation**, the company that actually does the credit scoring.

Here are a couple of common questions I get from audiences when I speak:

Should I save for retirement or should I save for my kids' college education?

Yes, I know some of you don't have children yet and may be thinking this is a silly question, but for those who do, it is very relevant. Almost every month, you have to decide which should I save for. My flippant answer is "save for both." But I know that is just not feasible for some of you, at least not yet.

The real answer is retirement. You can take a loan out for your college education, or your children can. And that loan, by the way, can be relatively inexpensive compared to other kinds, like a personal loan.

Most borrowing rates for student loans are much lower than the going rate for a credit card or a personal loan, and even similar to a mortgage loan which, by the way, is collateralized by the real estate it purchased. In 2018, the direct undergraduate student loan interest rate was 5.05 percent, while the average mortgage loan rate was 4.82 percent. The average credit card rate was 16 percent and personal loans ranged from 8–15 percent.

Should I consolidate my credit card balances into a lower interest rate card, or just set up a plan to pay down my debt as quickly as possible?

If you have read the whole book to this point, you must know: I am not about establishing rules. Each circumstance is different. First of all, what is the interest rate you are paying on your various credit card bills?

I had one client who had some rates that were more than 15 percent, but others that were under 10 percent. He clearly was going to have a hard time earning more than 15 percent every year on his investments. Thus, those higher interest rate cards should be the ones consolidated into a lower rate or balance transfer card. A balance transfer card usually has a very low rate; some even have a zero interest rate for a period of time as long as twelve or eighteen months. This allows you some 'breathing room' to come up with the money to pay back the amount outstanding.

Having said this, it doesn't mean you should not pay your debt down as soon as possible. This chapter talks about the doubling-down method for paying off your expenses as quickly as possible so that the high interest cards are eliminated within twelve months. Do that too!

> **Key Points from Part 2, Chapter 2**
>
> - Credit is based on "Man's Confidence in Man!"
>
> - Is credit good or bad? It depends! It hinges on how you are using it and what your return is on the credit you use. Remember my business use of credit in which my earnings exceeded my credit costs. That is a great use of credit. But if my earnings never exceed my credit costs, that is not a good use of credit.
>
> - Remember the five most important factors in your credit score: (1) your payment history; (2) outstanding debt; (3) length of credit history; (4) accounts in use; and (5) inquiries and new accounts.
>
> - Find out your credit score by going to your Discover Card statement or visiting: www.annualcreditreport.com or www.myfico.com.

3

Rule #8: Can You Really Do It Yourself (DIY)?

"Invest in things you know about,"— Peter Lynch

"I'm not good with money. And I'm terrible with math. I barely got through my fifth-grade math class! How can I do investments?"

This is a quote from one of my potential clients. Are these limiting beliefs or empowering beliefs? Or are they truths?

What is a limiting belief? It is a belief that doesn't serve you, a belief that doesn't help you achieve your goals, your dreams and your desires. Do you believe that rich people are lucky and have some special skill or talent? If you do, you will definitely find it hard to become rich. You completely miss the fact that many rich people are not very intelligent, and others are not skillful or talented at all.

Do you believe that you must be excellent in math to be a great investor? Isn't this another limiting belief? I know some investors who have just looked at the price chart of stocks and prophesied that the stock was going to be a home run—and amazingly enough—they were right.

One audience member at a recent speech I gave recounted a story about his wife being enamored with a new computer she got in the late 1990s. He researched it a little bit and saw that sales were growing quite rapidly, though their earnings had not yet taken off. The couple decided to buy one hundred shares of the company. Were they excellent statisticians? No. But they did buy Apple Inc. (AAPL) and those hundred shares are worth two hundred times what they paid for them twenty years ago.

Now, if you are making similar statements about money and your math ability and say. "yes, that is true," I will say it is just a belief that either you were taught or someone told you—once—that has now become your mantra. And, it is clearly not serving you.

As Peter Lynch, the amazingly talented mutual fund manager of Fidelity Magellan in the 1980s stated in his best-selling book, *One Up on Wall Street,* "All the math you need in the stock market you get in the fourth grade."

Or maybe you believe that others are supposed to manage your money?

"Well, aren't they?"

I've heard that comment again and again.

I've also heard this:

"How can I watch my money? I have a full-time job. I work at least ten hours a day and I often work weekends. I barely have time to spend with my family. I can't spend my free time managing my money! I'm not really interested in the markets anyway!"

Is this you? Or someone you know well? A spouse or partner?

What do these statements mean?

Let's analyze them:

First of all, this person truly *believes* they have to work hard to make money instead of having their money work for them. This is a limiting belief that rich people know is false. The rich have their money work hard so they don't have to.

Having limited time is something I hear all the time. But what are you spending eight to ten hours a day doing? Do you check social media like Facebook or Instagram or SnapChat ten times a day for five or six minutes each? Well, that is an hour a day! How much time do you spend doing that?

How much time do you spend playing games every day? Or watching television? I know less and less people are watching TV, but what about Netflix or YouTube or other streaming shows?

If you want to be financially free, then spending time on "mind-numbing" activities is only setting yourself, your family, and your loved ones up for failure.

Mr. Lynch also makes an important point that you won't hear from any investment bank, commercial bank, insurance company or other professional asset management firm like those pesky mutual funds. He said, "Between the chance of making an unusually large profit on an unknown company and the assurance of losing only a small amount on an established company, the normal mutual fund manager, pension-fund manager or corporate portfolio manager would jump at the latter. Success is one thing, but it's more important not to look bad if you fail … you'll never lose your job losing your client's money in IBM." Of course, Peter made this statement in the 1990s before IBM actually became a 'risky' investment because computer hardware companies may actually lose money. Today, "desktop" computers are exceedingly rare, even in major corporations. And IBM is actually more of a services company consulting to the industry rather than selling a product with declining demand.

Peter also tells the truth about mutual fund managers when he states something no professional investor wants you to hear: "Fund managers spend a quarter of their working hours explaining what they just did—first to their immediate bosses in their own trust department, and then to their ultimate bosses … clients." He goes on to confirm what I also learned as a professional investor at both Citigroup and my own fund. Restrictions and regulations hamper results: the Securities and Exchange Commission (SEC) requires a fund to own no more than 10 percent of the shares in any given company. And the SEC requires funds to invest no more than 5 percent of the fund's assets in any one stock. We had similar rules at both Citigroup and SaLaurMor Capital which stopped me from being concentrated. Thus, my highest conviction ideas which should have produced outsized returns for my fund were weakened by the other investments. Thus, I made less money for my investors.

Funds have built-in handicaps that individuals don't have, and thus, individuals should outperform the professionals who are effectively fighting a boxing match with at least one, and sometimes two hands tied behind their back. Could you knock down Creed if both hands were tied behind his back? What if he also had to hop since he had a leg tied as well? This is what many huge mutual funds have to deal with. They must have a lot of energy to move their return even a little.

One key question I get asked is: **Should I invest in mutual funds at all?**

Well, read on to Chapter 4 of this section: "My Proprietary Stock Screen." But, to answer the question quickly, I believe you can do it all yourself. I do understand many of you just won't do it. And you will want to invest in stocks through funds.

I then highly recommend using passive management, not active. The difference is that passive management is investing in an index. That is, the fund simply replicates the index by investing in all five hundred stocks of the Standard and Poor's 500, if it is an S&P 500 fund. Or the index fund replicating the Dow Jones Industrial Average by investing in the thirty stocks in that index. And so on. Obviously, there are many different indices, including international funds, and there are even real estate, commodity, currency, and bond index funds.

Since the index funds just represent the overall index and are essentially run by computer programs, their expense ratio or cost to invest is very low. Generally, the S&P 500 index fund costs less than twenty basis points or 0.2 percent, while many actively managed funds cost two hundred basis points (2 percent) or more. The result is that if you were to invest $100 a month in each fund and assume an 8 percent annual return in each, the difference just because of the expenses would be about $25,000 after twenty-five years. Wouldn't you prefer to have that in your pocket and not the fund companies'?

There is a big assumption in the above example. It assumes that the returns of an actively managed fund and the passive fund are exactly the same. Of course, we know that less than one in four actively managed funds outperforms a passive fund over time. Thus, besides the expense hit, your return is likely to be lower than the average 8 percent return as well, if you invest in an actively managed mutual fund.

In his amazing *New York Times* best seller, *I Will Teach You To Be Rich*, Ramit Sethi explains that "All our lives, we've been taught to defer to experts: teachers, doctors, and investment 'professionals.' But ultimately, expertise is about results ... In our culture of worshipping experts, what have the results been? When it comes to finances in America, they've been pretty dismal." In fact, in a study given to high school seniors, only 33 percent of the questions were answered currently. Ramit goes on to say that "financial experts—in fact, fund managers and anyone who attempts to predict the market—are often no better than amateurs. They're often worse. The vast majority of twenty-somethings can earn more than the so-called 'experts' by investing on their own. No financial adviser. No fund manager ..."

Ramit goes on to state that "Most young people don't need a financial adviser ... Plus, financial advisers don't always look out for your interests. They're supposed to help you make the right decisions about your money, but keep in mind that they're actually not obligated to do what's best for you. Some of them will give you very good advice, but many of them are pretty useless. If they're paid on commissions, they usually will direct you to expensive, bloated funds to earn their commissions."

In his controversial book, *Millionaire Fastlane*, MJ DeMarco states one anchor to people on the "Sidewalk" is to allow others to manage your money. He defines these people as those who are one step away from being broke; those who don't have a plan; any found money is immediately spent; they have the mentality that everything bad happens to them and they should live for today because life's too short to plan for the future. And he goes on to say that this mindset allows you to play the victim. As in, "well, my financial advisor put my money in *that* fund that dropped 50 percent in 2008 and took six years to recover."

As DeMarco says, "You can't be a victim if you don't relinquish your power to someone capable of making you a victim." These are powerful words. I recommend you read that sentence again.

What have you given up responsibility for in your life? Isn't it time to reclaim it?

Sethi also states that "Being rich is within your control, not some expert's. How rich you are depends on the amount you're able to save and on your investment plan. But acknowledging this fact takes guts, because it means admitting that there's no one else to blame if you're not rich—no advisers, no complicated investment strategy, no 'market conditions.' But it also means you control exactly what happens to you and your money over the long term."

I completely agree with these sentiments!

You can easily start investing with a small amount of money. Many brokerage houses like TD Ameritrade and fund complexes like Vanguard have lowered their minimum amounts to invest. They are now competing with companies like Acorns. With this brokerage company, you can invest small amounts. However, let's be clear they charge a minimum of $1 per month. If you are only going to invest $10 a month, that is a 10 percent expense charge—way too high.

Clearly, to me at least, the amount which makes sense for the minimum Acorns account, is $200 a month—then the monthly fee is 0.5 percent. The problem with all Acorns accounts is you are still giving up responsibility for managing your money. The Acorns account is determining what portfolio you should invest in—what stocks, etc. You don't get to decide. When you open up your own account at Vanguard or TD Ameritrade you have full control and you make the decisions what to invest in. As of 2019, TD Ameritrade and Schwab do not have a minimum amount to put in your account to invest in stocks, but if you want to use leverage—a margin account—TD Ameritrade requires $2,000; Vanguard has a minimum of $1,000 to open an account.

I tell people if you are not interested in investing in the stock market, then find something you are interested in. It doesn't have to be shares that create your financial freedom. It could be rental income from real estate, or an Amazon fulfillment business or an EBay product fulfillment business. It could be developing a platform on YouTube or a following on Instagram. It might be franchising or trading currencies or commodities. There are literally hundreds of ways to make money. The methods are only limited by your imagination. What about starting a YouTube channel and getting advertisers?

Don't limit yourself. I recommend this affirmation from Sandy Forster's *How to Be Wildly Wealthy Fast*: "I am unlimited. I flood my mind, body and soul with prosperity consciousness ..." (see Appendix for the complete abundance affirmation).

To conclude, with more from Ramit: "It's not easy to learn that reliance on so-called 'experts' is largely ineffective ... Even though you'd think they'd know better, fund managers also fall prey to financial hype. You can see this in the trading patterns of funds themselves: Mutual funds 'turn over' stocks frequently, meaning they buy and sell funds a lot. The managers chase the latest hot stock, confident of their abilities to spot something that millions of others have not. What's more, they also demand extraordinary compensation." Get this: in 2017, the average Goldman Sachs (GS) employee made almost $400,000. That's the average! Despite this crazy amount of compensation, "fund managers from all companies still fail to beat the market 75 percent of the time."

One question that I have heard asked of many financial advisers and planners is:

Would you recommend passive or actively managed mutual funds?

This is another question that starts with the assumption that you won't be managing your money. I do recommend doing it yourself, as I stated in this chapter. But let's say your passion is real estate. You want to put some money into the stock market as well, and you don't want to use the proprietary stock screen in "My Proprietary Stock Screen" from the next chapter.

Passive or index stock funds have very low expenses (and expense ratios) and, in fact, some mutual fund companies have cut their ratio to less than 10 basis points (0.1 percent). This will significantly increase your return. Suppose the passive fund generates an 8 percent return for twenty years on a gross basis, so the net return after expenses is 7.95 percent (this example assumes a 5 basis points or 0.05 percent expense ratio) and you put $10,000 a year ($800 a month) into the fund. At the end of the twenty years, you would have about $455,000. Now suppose you put the same $10,000 into an actively managed fund. The average fund expense ratio was about 100 bps or one percent. Now, assume the actively managed fund generated the same 8 percent return for twenty years on a gross basis; the net return would be 7 percent. It must be noted, however, that 90 percent of actively managed funds have under-performed the market index over the last ten years

But importantly, your amount would only be about $410,000, or $45,000 less than the index fund. That is the power of compound interest combined with a higher expense ratio. If you must give up responsibility, give it up to an index fund, not an actively managed large capitalization mutual fund; that is my recommendation.

Another common question I hear financial advisers and planners answer— incorrectly most of the time, I have to admit—is:

Should I buy term insurance, universal life, or a whole-life insurance policy?

Just as I am not licensed to manage your money, I am not licensed to sell you insurance. And this question is very difficult to answer since I don't have all your information. Some key questions that should be answered:

- Are you married? If so, does your spouse/partner make less or more than you?

- Do you have children or other dependents who would need income support if you were to die? If not, life insurance is likely unnecessary.

- What is your current savings level, in and out of retirement funds?

- What is your current income level?

- What is your current disposable income?

- How old are you?

- How old are your dependents? Even if you do have children, if they are already out of college and working, it's unlikely you need to have life insurance to ensure they have support.

I have also heard this question from audiences often:

If get my retirement plan set up as a self-directed IRA, can I forward that money to you to help manage it?

Currently (in 2018), I am not licensed to manage your money. I am working as a prosperity coach. I do know plenty of financial advisers and planners who would gladly take your money—for a fee—and invest it for you.

However, assuming you did not just skip to this question, and you read the next chapter, "My Proprietary Stock Screen," you will see the process to invest in stocks. Further, in Chapter 6, you will see the procedure to invest in real estate.

Consider what resonates with you. Giving up responsibility to someone else is not what I recommend. Take responsibility for your life and your money. You can do it. It's not hard—unless you believe it's hard (and that is a limiting belief, isn't it?).

Finally, if you still want to use a financial adviser, even after reading this chapter, then read on:

Do you work with financial advisors to help them with their clients' money mindset?

The simple answer is yes. But listen to this scenario:

"Sell them all!"

"What?"

"You heard me! Sell all my stocks! I'm done with the stock market. It's too risky for me. I'm now down, what, 30 percent for the year? This is my life savings and I only have ten years to retirement. Sell them all!"

Financial advisors get these kind of calls all the time, especially when the market is going down.

How do they respond?

As part of my coaching, I help financial advisors with their clients' fears and subconscious beliefs around money.

What questions do financial advisors ask their clients to get a better idea of their risk tolerance and money blocks? And are these questions asked regularly—at least once a year?

Here is one:

Which of the following do you believe to be true?

1. Rich people are criminals.

2. There is never enough.

3. The rich get richer and the poor get poorer.

4. Not everyone can get rich.

5. Money is the root of all evil.

6. You can't be spiritual and rich.

7. Money is not for people like us.

8. You must work hard to make money.

Some financial advisers' clients agree with #6. If this is the case and they believe themselves to be spiritual ("a good soul" one client said), they have an internal conflict that can self-sabotage them from becoming rich. This is also the case if they answered "true" to #1 or #5. Believe it or not, some people have responded "true" to #1 and others have responded that #5 is true.

If a financial advisor's client believes "money is the root of all evil" or "rich people are criminals," but they also believe they are a "good" person who has high ethical standards, then they have an internal conflict.

Either the client doesn't become rich because they believe they have a "good soul," or they become rich and a criminal! The latter is unlikely to occur, and then they end up wondering why they are continually telling their advisor to sell at the lows and buy at the highs.

Financial advisors can easily convince their clients that these statements are not true by giving them the many examples of rich people who have contributed to charitable organizations or those who have become members of the "99 percent club." I have personally found rich people to be the most giving, caring, thoughtful, and spiritual people I know.

And financial advisers can obviously point out that when their clients become financially free and are worth $10,000,000, they can support their favorite charity and maybe even be the reason why cancer or heart disease is cured.

In the example above, I tell the financial advisors I help that this person has been brought up with a "poverty consciousness" rather than "prosperity consciousness." I define poverty consciousness as a person who focuses on the downside risk rather than the upside potential.

Rather than saying, "lucrative opportunities will come my way," they state, "I could lose all my money in this investment." They resent rich and successful people rather than admiring them. They tend to associate with other poverty-conscious individuals. And they believe that life happens to them, instead of believing that they create their own lives. These folks tend to blame their financial advisors for not being rich, rather than taking responsibility for their own circumstances compared to those who are prosperity conscious.

I recommend financial advisors go through their list of clients and determine which bucket they are in. If they are poverty conscious, what can the financial advisor do to move them toward prosperity consciousness?

The first step is to determine if they are open to change. Are they teachable? Are they coachable?

Advisors can determine this by asking them: 'What are you willing to give up to learn some new concepts?' If they say, "I am absolutely teachable," but you ask them to give up their favorite TV show or their weekly golf game to learn something new, and they say, "No way," then they really aren't teachable.

Once the financial advisor determines that they are teachable, they can discuss with them the fact that the client has certain limiting beliefs around money that are not serving them. The clients should know that their beliefs create their thoughts, which then create experiences that perpetuate and reinforce their beliefs. Then beliefs only get stronger. To master their thoughts, and therefore their life and destiny, they must first master their beliefs.

The way financial advisors can help their clients change their limiting beliefs to empowering beliefs around money so that they can take prudent risks, is by teaching them about affirmations (see the Appendix for some of my current favorites). Instead of them believing that the stock market is risky and "I can lose all my money," why not have them say each morning, "Money comes easily and frequently"? Or, "I am an excellent money manager!"

To conclude, financial advisors must consider whether their clients are underinvested in the stock market. Do they have 20 percent, 30 percent, 40 percent or more in liquid risk-free assets such as: checking accounts, savings accounts, certificate of deposits, money market, or short-term bond funds?

If so, does the financial advisor know why?

Perhaps they were taught about money growing up, and they didn't even know it. Their parents told them: "We can't afford that. That's too expensive," or, "You need to work hard to be rich and successful," or, "You should save for a rainy day!"

If money was a big struggle growing up or they had a parent whose money personality type was a protectionist[4], it's likely their money beliefs are limiting, not empowering.

> **Key Points from Part 2, Chapter 3**
>
> - You don't need an MBA or even a college degree to generate a sizable income from investing.
>
> - It only takes a third-grade education to become an investor. The math that is needed is division and multiplication, addition and subtraction. You can do this!
>
> - Take responsibility for your life. Even if you currently have a financial advisor or financial planner managing your money, you chose that person. So, you can't say, "Well, they lost me money." Well, no ... *you* lost it by making the decision to give it to them. I take full responsibility for all my investments (see my story about Black Warrior in Part 2, Chapter 4).

---

4. These people think that money is a rare commodity and they must protect theirs. They are constantly worried about it and they know that unforeseen circumstances can destroy it in a nanosecond. They're quicker to say "no" than "yes" to financial decisions and will often veto their partner when it comes to doing anything other than saving their money.

- Do you know how much time mutual fund and hedge fund managers actually spend analyzing and investing your money rather than doing other things (like compliance, marketing, meeting with existing investors)? From my experience, it is even less than the 75 percent that Peter Lynch quoted in the late 1990s. The amount of compliance activities have gone up dramatically in the last twenty years and at least 50 percent of my time was spent not investing. I would expect this is similar for mutual fund managers in 2019.

- What type of investment are you interested in? It doesn't have to be stocks! Is it real estate? A side business? Currency-trading? Figure out where your interest lies, what your belief level is (see Part 1, Chapter 2: "When You Believe"), and what your intuition is telling you. Go there.

- Do it yourself!

4

My Proprietary Stock Screen

"For some reason the whole business of analyzing stocks has been made to seem so esoteric and technical that normally careful consumers invest their life savings on a whim." — Peter Lynch in *One Up On Wall Street*

"Hey Joel. It's Mike. Black Warrior Resources!"

"What is that?"

"Oh. It's the next great idea I have for you!"

"Can it work?"

"Oh definitely. There are a limited number of these out there. No one knows about it. It trades for just over a $1 and when they discover oil on their territory, it will jump to at least $5 and maybe even $10. How much do you have to invest?"

"Well, I don't know. What if they don't discover oil."

"Well, it can't go much lower. It's just over a $1!"

"Okay. Well, I have $1,000 to spare right now."

"Great. Send me a check or I can pick it up from you. Are you still living in Merrick?"

"I'll send you the check. How many shares should we buy?"

"I'd buy as many as possible. Can you do 1,000 shares? That's only $1,300 all in."

"okay Thanks."

This is a conversation I had with my stockbroker in 1988. My first and only stockbroker! He was a friend of a friend. Like many great salesmen, he sold me on the opportunity. I could make five to ten times my money! I was sold on the idea of wealth!

Did I do any research? Did I ask the appropriate questions? Did I ask:

1. What is the probability of it hitting five dollars in the next three years?

2. What is the probability of it hitting ten dollars in the next three to five years?

3. What is the downside and what is that probability?

4. How much money does the company make (its net income or operating income)?

5. What are its sales?

6. Has it discovered oil before?

7. Who runs the company? Do they own stock? Are they buying more?

8. Who are their competitors?

9. What is the profit margin (its income divided by its sales)? Has it been increasing or decreasing?

10. How can I read about the company? Is there a report you can send me? (of course these days, you would just go to the company website and read about it).

Now, these are just a few questions I didn't ask.

What happened to Black Warrior? Well, my last memory of it was when I called up that same stockbroker and asked him how I should record a stock that has been delisted on my tax return! The company went bankrupt and I lost my $1,300.

Yes, invest in what you know. Why do we think that we have to invest in some newfangled (that is a technical term) business to make money—to make our money work for us?

Here is a simple screen I have my clients use to determine whether a stock is worth investigating further. Some only use the screen to invest; it can work, but I recommend doing a little more analysis than that. You can even call the company's investor relations department or email them and ask the ten questions above.

Consider this: your daughter is only shopping at American Eagle Outfitters (AEO) because it has the coolest fashions for teenagers. Wouldn't you want to check quickly to see if it is worth investing in rather than just going to the store and seeing it really busy every Saturday afternoon? Absolutely you would.

So, here is a simple screen to use. It is only five steps, and it will definitely give you a sense if more investigation is worthwhile and the stock is likely to move up. If the stock meets all the criteria (i.e., all the answers are "yes" or "true"), then you proceed.

Before I introduce the stock screen, I want to define some terms to make the process easier to understand (for those expert stock investors, you can skip ahead a page).

First, let's start with market capitalization or "market cap." This is the value of the company that the stock market has assigned to that company. The shares or stock outstanding is the amount of stock or shares that the company has issued.

The earnings or profit or net income is the amount of money that the company has earned. It could be for the quarter or the year. When an analyst or investor quotes "earnings per share" or "EPS," this means the amount of money the company has made, divided by the outstanding shares.

Now, earnings can be net income or operating income or an adjusted measure. Some companies adjust each quarter's earnings for 'one-time' items that are not supposed to occur again, but invariably do! For simplicity sake, we will use operating income for the companies in the screen—taking out one-time items or capital gains/losses for companies that invest in securities.

Revenues is another important term that I use in the stock screen. It is just how much of the product was sold by the company in the quarter. For an insurance company, I use earned premiums: the amount of premiums that the company reported for that quarter.

To be clear, the price or "P" in the ratios below is just the market capitalization of the stock divided by the shares outstanding. The "E" is the earnings per share or EPS.

If the P/E is 10, you would expect the company to be growing at 10 percent per year—forever.

The profit margin is the amount of profit per dollar of sales or revenues of the company. If the company is making more money per sale this quarter compared to last quarter or will have a higher profit margin next year versus this year, that is good news for investors.

It means that if they sell the same amount, they will actually make more money. Wouldn't you like to have that!

Here are the stock screen steps:

1. Calculate the most recent quarter's earnings per share growth and see if the EPS growth is more than 10 percent. Let's use Amazon as an example. For the second quarter of 2018, AMZN had EPS of $5.07, and in the second quarter of 2017, it reported EPS of $1.25. Thus, its EPS growth was 306 percent (5.07/1.25 - 1). Is the growth in EPS more than 10 percent? Yes!

2. Calculate the most recent quarter's sales growth and see if it is more than 5 percent. Continuing to use Amazon as an example, for the second

quarter of 2018, AMZN had sales of $52.9 billion (bn). For the second quarter of 2017, AMZN reported sales of $38 bn. Thus, the growth was 39 percent (52.9/38). Is the growth in sales more than 5 percent? Yes!

3. Is the number in (1) higher than (2)? Sure it is. This is checking if the profit margin is increasing, and it is in this case—so, that is a good thing!

4. Calculate the current P/E (using the earnings just reported) and forward P/E based on next year's earnings expectations and check: Is the growth in EPS more than the P/E? "P" is the stock's price. AMZN was trading at $1,808 at the close of business on July 26, 2018, when it reported its earnings. So, its P/E was 89.2 (1808/(4 × 5.07)). I used a multiplier of four for the earnings in the quarter of $5.07, because we want to see what the P/E for four quarters of earnings (a full year). To be clear, most analysts use the "TTM" or Trailing Twelve Month's earnings as the denominator in any P/E calculation, since earnings may be seasonal. Seasonal means that a company may make more money in a particular quarter like the one ending December 31st if they are a retailer and sell a lot of toys for Christmas. AMZN's forward 2019 P/E was 71.3 (1808/25.37 - 1). The $25.37 is the average earnings estimate for 2019 by the professional analysts who project AMZN's earnings for next year. In this case, the EPS growth was 306 percent, which is higher than the P/E (take out the percent) based on the current quarter and the forward earnings. So, *is* the growth in EPS more than the P/E? Yes!

5. Check how the stock performed on the day of earnings on an absolute basis and compared to the overall stock market. Did the stock go up on its earnings report? On July 26, 2018, AMZN stock declined about 3 percent. On that day, the overall stock market (as represented by the Standard and Poor's 500) declined about twenty-five basis points (0.25 percent). On a relative and absolute basis, AMZN stock declined. So, the answer here is: no!

Does AMZN meet all criteria? Well, it's close, but, no, it did not meet all five items. So, we would not invest in this stock after that earnings report. As of this writing, AMZN stock is down about 26 percent from the day-before earnings, while the overall stock market is down 17 percent. So, on both an absolute basis (-26 percent) and relative basis (-26 percent less 17 percent = -9 percent), we made a very good decision not to purchase AMZN on the day after its second-quarter earnings report.

Step 5 in the screen is a market indicator. The only one of the five steps that is. Its purpose is to determine if the company positively or negatively surprised investors (or potential investors) in its quarterly report. In this case, it appeared the stock market was expecting better performance despite the very, very strong earnings and revenue growth that AMZN reported. AMZN is discussed more in the next chapter, including why it has been a truly revolutionary investment and company since 1999.

Importantly, some long-term investors will not use Step 5, because it is just the current holders of the stock (and those who are short) making an investment decision that day. If you are a long-term investor with strong conviction (see Part 1, Chapter 2: "When You Believe") that Amazon is a great investment idea, you won't be swayed by the movement of the stock on one particular day. However, in the case of Amazon, it stopped us from investing in a company that dropped 26 percent, avoiding a big loss.

Before we move on to Rule #9: "Don't Diversify," I wanted to define some other key terms I look at when analyzing a company. Some readers may find this valuable information, but it is not absolutely essential to make a lot of money in the stock market.

Book value is the accounting value of the company. When an investor goes to the balance sheet of the company and sees the words "shareholders' equity," that is the total value of the company. When you divide this amount by the outstanding shares, the term is called book value. This is just the accounting value of the company per share.

I usually compare this amount to the market capitalization or price. If the price is a lot higher than the book value, then stock market investors are attributing a lot more value to the company than its accounting value. The company may have hidden assets like extra reserves set aside for future claims that actually don't materialize (like the best insurers I know), or they may have invested in real estate that has appreciated over ten, twenty, or thirty years. They might well have "franchise value" or a brand that is very valuable like Google (GOOG) or Coca-Cola (KO) or McDonalds (MCD).

Another item I look at is the company's net cash position. Like an individual's balance sheet, I like to see if they have more cash than debt. An investor can look at the balance sheet of the company, add up their cash and short-term assets, and then subtract their short-term debt and long-term debt. If it is positive, that is a good attribute. Now if you divide this amount by the shares outstanding, you get a per share amount.

Suppose the company had $5 per share of cash. If the stock is trading at just $4, you know you have a real bargain. Even if the stock is at $6, it is likely to be very cheap because the stock market is only attributing $1 ($6–$5) to the value of all its future profits and other assets.

As a former credit analyst, I would be remiss if I didn't talk more about debt and credit (see Part 2, Chapter 2 for a discussion on credit: "Should I Use Credit?" as it pertains to individuals). How much money the company owes is a critical factor. I compare total debt to equity. I wouldn't invest in a company that has more debt than equity, and for most regulated companies, like insurers, the amount of debt is generally 20–50 percent of their equity.

Another way to check the riskiness of a company is to look at how much interest they are paying on the debt it has outstanding compared to earnings. Let's go back to Amazon. In the second quarter of 2018, the company reported interest expense of $343 million. Its earnings before taxes were $2,605 million. Thus, its earnings before interest and taxes (EBIT) was $2,948 ($2,605+$343) million. So it covered its interest payments by 8.6 ($2,605 million divided by $343 million) times. This is a very strong number. Based on its earnings for the quarter, AMZN could pay almost nine years of interest.

Finally, some investors will only purchase stocks that pay a dividend. This amount is simply a payment to investors each quarter. I don't go this far, but it is a conservative way to invest.

Think about it, with the 10-year Treasury note at slightly less than 3 percent in the fourth quarter of 2018 (and below 2.5 percent in the first quarter of 2019), why wouldn't you just buy all the stocks in the market that pay a dividend every year of 5 percent—especially if the company has a history of increasing its dividend every year?

The reason is, if the stock goes down just 5 percent, then you break even. And if the stock drops more, you lose money. There is still risk in owning a dividend-paying stock, but a dividend will give you what I call downside protection. It is unlikely that a stock that is paying a 5 percent dividend and has a history of increasing that dividend, will drop 50 percent, because then it would be yielding more than 10 percent next year which investors would find too enticing. They would then bid up the stock price, thus, it would be unlikely to drop the full 50 percent.

As the reader knows, I don't like rules. The stock screen is just one way to determine whether a stock should be considered a potential investment. There are hundreds, if not thousands, of ways to invest in stocks (and other markets for that matter) and no one method is right or wrong. They are just perspectives and opportunities to make money.

In fact, I know one speculator who rarely knows anything about a company, but he uses technical analysis to determine if the stock is a *buy* or a *sell*. Technical analysis looks only at the price of the stock and the volume (how many shares are traded on a particular day) to determine its future price movement.

So, know there are many ways to make money in the stock market and other markets (see Part 2, Chapter 6: "Real Estate Can Make You Rich!"), but remember how important your belief system is, as well as your intuition and faith.

Aren't stocks risky?

This is a question a client asked me before I began my lesson on shares. This is a fear-based question. First of all, how do you define *risky*? I will tell you that I know plenty of people who became financially free and/or made millions of dollars in the stock market. They had a long-term time horizon (not 3-6 days or weeks!) and were being mindful—they had a plan. They executed this plan when the average investor got emotional. They had a strong conviction level (aka a very high belief level—Rule #1) in each investment idea.

If the upside potential is 100 percent and the downside risk is 20 percent, is that stock risky? Yes, if you need the stock appreciation to pay for food for the next week. Then I would highly recommend not investing in this stock or the stock market in general. In that case, I would not call it *investing*. I would call it *speculating* or *betting*. Time horizon plays a key role in your investments, as does belief level. Know what your time horizon is, and what your belief level is *before* you invest. And have a plan in place when the inevitable price drop in your investment happens. Will you buy more, stay on the sidelines, or sell it all?

Key Points from Part 2, Chapter 4

- You should know some basic terms before you invest.
- Know the key terms for stock market investors:
    1. operating income
    2. market capitalization (market cap)
    3. revenues (aka sales)
    4. Price/Earnings (P/E)
    5. Book Value (BV)
    6. Earnings Before Interest and Taxes (EBIT)

- Know the five-step process for stock investing and use it for all your security selections:

  1. Calculate the growth in EPS year-over-year for the current quarter. Check if it is more than 10 percent. If it is, go to step #2.

  2. Calculate the growth in revenues year-over-year for the current quarter. Check if it is more than 5 percent. If it is, go to step #3.

  3. Check if the amount in step #1 is more than step #2. If so, continue to step #4.

  4. What is the current P/E of the stock? If it is less than step #1, go to step #5.

  5. Check how the stock did the day it reported earnings. Did the stock appreciate more than the overall stock market? If yes, you might have a winner!

- Consider other factors such as the company's debt level, interest coverage, and dividend rate when investing in stocks.

5

Rule #9: Don't Diversify

"The whole secret of successful investing is non-diversification. If you know nothing, diversify!" — Charlie Munger, Chairman of Berkshire Hathaway whose net worth is about $2 billion as of this writing.

"You want me to put *all* my money into what company? What? A company named after a rainforest in South America? Why? What does it do?

"It sells books over the internet."

"Really. Just books. Who cares? How big can that be?"

"Well, there are over three billion books that are read every year! Imagine if they get a 10 percent share of that!"

"Okay, okay. How much is it up over the last year? I know internet stocks have done really well in the last few years."

"True. It is up almost ten times in the last year. But it really does have a great business model!"

"Ten times ... really. And you think it has *more* upside? Call when you have something of real value to discuss."

This is a fictitious conversation that an investor had with his broker in January 1999. What was the company, you might ask!

It was Amazon (AMZN) of course. And, for those who invested $10,000 that day in early 1999 at $10, they would have over $1,915,000, as of September 2018. That is an annualized return of 30 percent per year!

Remember this was less than a year before internet stocks, in general, and Amazon, specifically, collapsed. It peaked at $75 in March of 2000 and dropped as low as $8.50 in 2001 before it began to recover. That means that any investor could have purchased it again in 2001 at a similar price to where it traded in 1999, and their annualized return would have been even higher—35 percent.

Would it have paid to diversify and invest in the whole Nasdaq index in mid-2001, instead of Amazon? No! Instead of multiplying your money by 190times, you would have multiplied your money by six times. You would have $60,000, not $1.9 million.

Let's first define diversification as it pertains to investing. According to Investopedia, diversification is the process of allocating capital in a way that reduces the exposure to any one particular asset or risk. A common path toward diversification is to *reduce risk or volatility* by investing in a variety of assets. If asset prices do not change in perfect synchrony, a diversified portfolio will have less variance than the weighted average variance of its constituent assets, and often less volatility than the least volatile of its constituents.

In layperson's terms, diversification is supposed to reduce your risk because you are investing in more than one asset and these assets generally will not move in a perfect relationship or correlation to each other.

It's been statistically proven that diversification is "good."

Harry Markowitz in a 1952 essay, established "Modern Portfolio Theory" (MPT), stating that an asset's risk and return should not be assessed by itself, but by how it contributes to a portfolio's overall risk and return. It uses the variability of asset prices as a "proxy" for risk. It is essentially a formalization and extension of diversification.

The central tenet of Markowitz's MPT is that all investors are "rational" and thus have an inherent negative bias to absorbing more risk without being adequately compensated by a higher return. This meant to Harry that for the average return, most investors will prefer to minimize the volatility of that return. Thus, he defined risk as the variability of returns.

Now, here is where diversification comes into play. Harry stated that investors will minimize the variability of their expected return by diversifying their selection of stocks—holding different types of securities (like bonds, stocks or real estate) or various companies. He also pointed out that by just holding a lot of different securities, your risk won't be reduced if they move together—they are highly correlated. Harry stated that effective diversification only happens when the stocks don't move together.

This theory contains a lot of assumptions. First, it assumes that all investors are "rational." What this means is that you won't act emotionally. But most investors do. And especially when they shouldn't, like in 2008 and 2009 during the Great Recession, or the crash in October of 1987.

Secondly, there are many ways to define risk, and of course, many different types of risk. Markowitz defines risk by variability of returns. But do I really care (is it really risk) when my stock moves up more than I expect it to?

Shouldn't we just look at "downside variability" of returns. In this case, the variability would be half!

Also, there are plenty of other types of risks. What about the risk of opportunity cost? That means, what if I put all my money in to a checking account at a bank, earnings essentially zero, and the stock market goes up 8 percent a year while I have that money in the bank. Is there risk associated with that? What if inflation is running 3 percent a year, and in twenty-four years (remember the "Rule of 72") my money is worth half on an inflation-adjusted basis.

Do you like risk? In Jordan Peterson's best seller, *12 Rules for Life*, he explains that kids love playgrounds, but more importantly they need playgrounds that are dangerous to be challenging. And most importantly, he states that "People (including children who are people too, after all) don't seek to minimize risk. They seek to optimize it. They don't drive and walk and love so that they achieve what they desire, but they push themselves a bit at the same time, too. So they continue to develop. We're hardwired for that reason to enjoy risk. Some of us more than others."

Are you hardwired to enjoy risk? Are you open to "making friends ... (learning) what you don't know, instead of what you do know?" Yes, risk can be defined many different ways. What is risky to you may not be considered to be a risk to others.

You have a limited amount of money to invest. So, you invest $5,000 in one great idea and a further $5,000 in another. As you only have $10,000 to invest in total, this is all of your investable cash. But then you do more research, and find another opportunity which appears to have similar upside (say you expect all three stocks to double) and limited downside (suppose you expect your loss to be limited to 10–15 percent).

What do you do?

Would you spend the money on commissions to sell $1,666 of your position in each of the first two stocks (so that you have $3,333.33 in each stock) or would you just keep the first two positions, since all three stocks have the same potential gain and loss?

Suppose you just keep the first two positions, and as expected, two years later, both have doubled and you now have $20,000. But what if the third position quadrupled, so that if you had invested in that stock, your total would be $26,666 (or a 167 percent gain instead of a 100 percent gain). See, there is an "opportunity cost risk" for not investing in a stock that does better than your portfolio. Recently, some professionals have started to call this FOMO—Fear Of Missing Out.

And consider two stocks: ABC has an average return of 25 percent and risk (also known as variability) of 15 percent, and XYZ has an average return of 10 percent and variability of 12 percent. According to Markowitz, ABC is more risky than XYZ, but ABC's return is very unlikely to go negative, while XYZ's will almost certainly go negative—at least one year assuming you hold it for, say, 25 years.

Also, Harry's construct doesn't take into account the fact that each investor can tolerate different amounts of risk.

Are you twenty-two, single, making $100,000 and have a net worth of $50,000 with no debt?

Or are you fifty-five, married, making $100,000 with a net worth of $50,000 and $200,000 of debt?

Who can take on more risk?

I would recommend the twenty-two-year-old take on more risk since they have a lot more time on their hands and no debt.

Markowitz himself, in *Portfolio Selection: Efficient Diversification of Investments*, states: "An investor who sought only to maximize the expected return **would never prefer a diversified portfolio**. If one security had greater expected return than any other, the investor would place all his funds in this security … Thus, if we consider diversification a sound principle of investment, we must reject the objective of simply maximizing expected return."

To put that into layperson's terms, Markowitz is saying that if all anyone wanted to do was to get the best return on their investments, then they would not diversify! Well said! And of course, I totally agree.

We started the chapter with Charlie Munger's quote, but some people know his CEO better. Charlie Munger has effectively worked side by side with Warren Buffett since 1978. Buffett said, "There are situations, for the full-time investor, where it'd be a mistake not to invest 50 percent of your net worth in one business."

Some people may not want to listen to Warren, but many others agree. In fact, Peter Lynch, who ran one of the most successful mutual funds in the 1980s and grew the assets under management from $20 million to over $14 billion (yes, that is a "b" not an "m'") when he left, had a lot of great thoughts regarding diversification, despite the fact that he managed a fund that at its peak had more than 1,500 stocks in it!

He said in his highly entertaining book, *One Up On Wall Street,* that "It's best to own as many stocks as there are situations in which (a) you've got an edge; and (b) you've uncovered an exciting prospect that passes all tests of research. Maybe that's a single stock, or maybe it's a dozen stocks ... There's no use diversifying into unknown companies, just for the sake of diversity. A foolish diversity is the hobgoblin of small investors."

Peter went on to state: "**In small portfolios [i.e., those I recommend for the readers of this book], I'd be comfortable owning between three and ten stocks**."

Peter also tells the story about how, when he took over Fidelity Magellan, the head of Fidelity, Ned Johnson, had recommended Peter cut the number of stocks in his portfolio from forty to twenty-five.

Another high-profile investor and highly regarded economist, John Maynard Keynes, stated, "One good share is safer than ten bad ones." Keynes also remarked that "To carry one's eggs in a great number of baskets, without having time or opportunity to discover how many [baskets] have holes in the bottom is the surest way of increasing risk and loss."

I know from my own experience at Citi and at SaLaurMor Capital as a hedge fund investor—managing more than $700 million at the peak—that my top five ideas made the large majority of our returns. When SaLaurMor Capital made 10 percent for its investors in 2013 in just over six months, our top five positions—out of an average of sixty—contributed more than 50 percent of the total return.

Before I discuss business owners, I'd like to be clear. To me, diversification means investing in a large number of stocks or bonds or real estate holdings—any security type. If I had just invested in my top ten ideas at Citi, we would have made a lot more money. My recommendation is to invest in a small number of securities that you feel *comfortable* with. What is your intuition telling you? Is five the right number, or eight or two? It shouldn't be ninety!

Some of you may be thinking this: "I've done my research; I have found this great idea and I know it's worth a lot more—maybe 5 times more—and I think the downside is only 30 percent. But I'm fifty years old and earn just $50,000. My life savings is $200,000. Should I put it all in this one investment?"

To me, there is no right answer. My response will differ depending on you!

What does your intuition say? What is your risk tolerance? If you invest all $200,000 in this investment, and it went down 20 percent within 3 months after you invested, would you care that you now only have $160,000 because you *know* the upside is now more than 6 times and the downside is just 12.5 percent? Maybe you would feel more comfortable putting $100,000 in right away, then waiting with the other $100,000 in case it dropped more than 10 percent, so that you can take advantage of the "lucrative opportunity" and buy more. Each person is different. Some may say "Wait! What if it goes up 50 percent tomorrow, then I've missed out on $50,000 (this is the FOMO—Fear Of Missing Out I mentioned earlier)." You must know your own risk tolerance, tax status, what other cash flow you have, other retirement savings, etc. There is no one right answer. You have to know yourself and have a plan for various situations. And trust your intuition (maybe re-read Part 1, Chapter 4!).

What about business holdings?

Do you believe Jeff Bezos, the CEO of Amazon (AMZN) as of this writing, believes in diversification? If you have a strong belief in your idea and the success of it, would you diversify and buy other retail companies? Would Jeff Bezos be worth more than $110 billion as of this writing if he did that?

The founder of a company doesn't say, "I am going to start twenty-five companies and be diversified in case one of them doesn't work out."

Consider the founder of Apple Inc., Steve Jobs. Yes, he had a lot of ups and downs and he did start another company, NeXT, after he was forced out of Apple, as well as what eventually became Pixar. But did he "diversify?"

I don't like to say "always" or "never," nor do I like to say "all" or "every." But almost every business leader I know does not diversify by investing in his competitors or other companies in his industry or another industry. They bet it all on their own company. Jamie Dimon, currently CEO of J.P. Morgan Chase (JPM), doesn't have his net worth tied up in hundreds of stocks. Jamie was worth more than $1 billion in the third quarter of 2018, because of his $9 million shares in Chase.

So, why do portfolio managers invest in hundreds of stocks and why do real estate investors invest in twenty or thirty properties or more?

Is it because of the past downturns that have occurred?

I believe so.

But is it also because of a fear of loss?

A fear that the stock is going to go down and they will lose money. Yes, again!

Another way to diversify is by asset class. That is, instead of putting all your money into stocks or real estate, you put some money into stocks, some into real estate, some into bonds, and some into cash.

The argument for diversifying by asset class is that you will get a higher "risk-adjusted return."

What does that mean?

Well, is it better to have an average 10 percent return with 1 percent volatility, or a 15 percent return with 1 percent volatility? Volatility is the rate at which the price of a security increases or decreases for a given return level. It is measured by calculating the standard deviation of the annualized returns over some period of time. It shows the range to which the price of a security may increase or decrease.

Clearly, you would prefer the higher return with the same amount of movement.

But what about a 15 percent return with 5 percent volatility vs. a 20 percent return with a 10 percent volatility. Academics will tell you that the risk-adjusted return is higher with the 15 percent, so invest in that mix of assets. But my personal belief is that this is based on fear. Fear that the volatility comes when you most need the money.

In layperson's terms, this means you could lose 20 percent of your money right when you are going to retire. And imagine having to take the money out of your account at that time! You have less than necessary to live on. But if you invest to win, you prefer an average return of 20 percent, no matter what the volatility is, compared to a 15 percent return, no matter what that volatility is.

Earl Nightingale said: "You get what you think about most of the time." If you are fearful of a big downturn right when you retire and you are focused on that, guess what is likely to happen?

Why not think about what you want to happen? And if you do invest in the higher return asset mix with higher volatility over the next five years, your return will be substantially higher and you might even be able to go to cash in five years. Because 20 percent compounded over five years is an almost 250 percent return, while a 15 percent return over five years is only a doubling of your investment; which would you rather have?

The general consensus is that you should invest in a certain percentage of stocks, like 70 percent, and a certain percentage in bonds, say 30 percent.

The percentage in stocks should decrease as you get older, and especially as you enter retirement age (sixty-five or so). But when you are sixty-five, your life expectancy in 2018 is nineteen years if you are a man, and over twenty-one years if you are a woman. Those are averages. Your probability of living to ninety is actually about 25 percent.

I tell my clients that everyone is different. It depends on their tax status, risk tolerance, earnings, cash flow, net worth, and health as to what percentage you should have in stocks. But the argument that you should be "diversified" is purely based on fear. A fear that your "overweight" asset class is going to go down.

One financial advisor told me it is "suicide" to have a client have all their investments in stocks at seventy-five. And yet a healthy retiree who doesn't drink and is in excellent health, has a twenty-year life expectancy at seventy-five.

If you aren't working, you still want your money working for you—and hard—over the next twenty years. Recall that twenty years is the average or median, and the probability of living to a hundred is over 20 percent.

Remember what Yuval Harari stated. The common myth is "diversification is good." I know I am not going to change the hundreds of millions of people who believe this. But it is certainly a limiting belief! If you were to invest more aggressively and achieve a 20 percent return vs. a 15 percent return, or a 15 percent return instead of 10 percent, would you be happier or scared?

How do you define risk? Is it truly more risky to be invested in a stock if you know you are going to make money based on your analysis? Would you care if it went down 10 percent or 20 percent (or more) in the next two or three years if your time horizon is ten years or more? I've had plenty of securities that I invested in go down before they went up and reach my price target. Avoid diversification and see your returns soar.

Key Points from Part 2, Chapter 5

- Concentrate your investments. The best business leaders do. They have confidence in their own companies and don't invest in twenty-five or fifty businesses in other industries. As Peter Lynch said, it is okay to have just a couple of handfuls of stocks. I would say the same about real estate investments (see the next chapter!). You don't need to have more than ten, especially if your conviction level (also known as your belief level) is an 8 or 9 or 10. Having just a few stocks or real estate investments makes sense. Don't let the 'professionals' tell you otherwise.

- Don't split your assets into different asset classes like stocks, bonds, cash, real estate, etc. because of a fear of loss.

- Have faith in your investments.

- Avoid "di-worse-ification!"

6

Real Estate Can Make You Rich!

Just like any investment, real estate *can* make you rich!

Do you believe? Go ahead, rate yourself on your belief scale from one to ten. Where are you? If you are higher than a seven read on. If not, then skip to the Conclusion. Really! Or reread Chapter 2: "When You Believe."

I am serious! If you have massive doubt or even a fairly high level of doubt that real estate can make you rich, then don't go there.

Okay. You have a high level of belief. Where do you start?

There are endless opportunities in both commercial and residential property; however, this chapter will only focus on residential income properties, as it is the most commonly available investment property type. Simply using the applications provided in this chapter can rapidly make you an expert in any market you choose.

If you do wish to invest in residential income property, the best thing you can do is to start in your own community and learn everything you can about the dynamics of property in your market (see #1 below). Many people spend time looking at real estate for sale online for fun and often don't realize that the information they find there is a first big step to learning about real estate.

The best way to start is by looking at the price per square foot (price per sf) of residential properties in your own neighborhood by using Zillow.com or Realtor.com. Look at houses that are for sale and those that have sold (comparable properties or peers). Look at the price per sf for each property and then actually visit the residences when they have open houses; you will soon find that pictures do not accurately depict the property. In time, you will become an expert simply by looking at the price per sf and by following sales as they occur.

With that knowledge, you'll now have a feel for the value in the market you are focused on. You may also want to know if these properties are good investments.

How to Analyze, Compare and Value Properties Using the Gross Rent Multiplier (GRM)

Next, you can estimate the gross rent that the property produces and apply a multiplier for the property in question. There is such a multiplier called the Gross Rent Multiplier (GRM). This amount relates rent and value.

To derive the GRM for your market, apply the following on properties that have sold:

Property value ÷ estimated gross rent (monthly rent × 12) = Gross Rent Multiplier (GRM)

To value an income property that you are considering buying, you can apply the GRM:

Estimated gross rent (monthly rent × 12) × Gross Rent Multiplier (GRM) = value

A higher-value property or market will have a higher GRM, and a lower-value property or market will have a lower GRM. This is a quick and easy 'back of the envelope' way to value income properties. It is easy to derive the GRM.

You can also use it to compare two income properties. However, GRM has its limitations. it does not account for the varying expenses of properties. One property may have significantly lower taxes, or the tenant can pay utilities in one property and the landlord in another. This sometimes leads to an "apples to oranges" comparison between properties you would like to buy because the bottom line will change. Therefore, the best metric to apply is one which takes into account both income *and* expenses.

For a stock, as stated in Part 2, Chapter 4: "My Proprietary Stock Screen," one characteristic of it being inexpensive is that its P/E is lower than its earnings growth (for the quarter or upcoming year).

A similar type of analysis can be done for your real estate investment. Remember, the P/E is the stock's value divided by its earnings. In real estate, one key term is the capitalization rate (aka cap rate), and it includes both income and expenses. This is the inverse of the P/E. Flip the P and the E so that you are calculating an E/P ratio). It is the ratio of the net operating income of the structure compared to the price, or the cost of buying the structure.

For example, in stocks, a P/E of less than ten times (10x) is usually considered cheap. Many financial stocks in 2018 were trading at less than 9x.

For real estate, a P/E of 10 would translate to a 10 percent cap rate (1/10 is 0.1 or 10 percent). And a P/E lower than 10, say 9x, like many financial stocks, would translate into an 11 percent cap rate (1/9 is 0.1111 or 11.11 percent).

The higher the capitalization rate, the lower P/E value.

It is interesting to note that the P in stocks is the current market value of the company. For real estate, the price of the structure is truly unknown until it is bought or sold. Many investors will use the cost of the property. But if the property has not transacted for many years, the cost will *not* equal the P (or price) when it is transacted next.

An example is my parent's house in Massapequa. They bought it in 1967 for $26,000. That is their initial cost. Now, even if you add the improvements they've made over the last fifty years, it only comes to $56,000.

Let's continue with our example. Suppose they wanted to rent out the house. It has five bedrooms and three bathrooms. The going rate in their area to rent would be approximately $3,500 a month, or $42,000 a year. That would be their gross income. Assuming a normal average annual vacancy rate (they won't have tenants every month of every year), insurance, utilities, normal repairs, and maintenance, their net operating income would be approximately $30,000. Since the house hasn't sold in fifty years, you will have to use peers for the value or price (like the "P" in the P/E ratio).

There are many houses for sale in the area. Using a peer group, the average house price is about $719,000. If we use a round number of $700,000, then the cap rate would be 4.3 percent.

Anyone buying the house for $700,000 assuming they can earn $30,000 in net operating income after expenses would not be getting a great deal.

Remember, a cap rate over 10 percent is generally considered cheap, and a cap rate below 10 percent is generally considered expensive. However, you know by now that I am not a rules person! This is not true all the time. There are times when a cap rate of 6 percent might be a great investment, and a property with a cap rate of 12 percent might be a terrible one. For example, suppose the economic area is about to start booming, like San Antonio a few years ago. The cap rates might have been 6 percent (somewhat expensive), but if you knew the house you purchased was going to appreciate 10 percent a year for five years, because of an economic boom, would this be a great investment? Of course!

Similarly, you might invest in a property that has a cap rate of 12 percent. Suppose you didn't take into consideration one-time expenses that will increase your repair and maintenance costs. Alternatively, the economy might be about to collapse. Say you purchased a home in Detroit in 2006 with a cap rate of 12 percent. The investment looked cheap, but the ability to sell the property over the next five years was limited.

Now, let's back up a bit and think about what characterizes a 'great' deal.

First, real estate for those of you who are believers is quite simple. You must be great at only three things:

- Finding cheap properties.

- Finding cheap financing (lenders willing to provide you the money to buy the property at a good rate).

- Selling the property at the right time—i.e., quickly, if you think the market is going to go down, or slowly, if you think the market is about to take off.

Here are some simple suggestions for people just starting out in real estate. Let's be clear—this doesn't apply to those of you who are already sophisticated real estate investors; these are suggestions, not rules:

1. Start with properties within a small distance from your house. Some suggest twenty-five miles, others say use fifty miles. I recommend whatever area you are most familiar with. If there are enough properties within ten miles, start there. Currently—in 2018—there are nineteen properties for sale in Rye Brook and another thirty in Port Chester (the town that Rye Brook split from in 1982). If I were to add in a few more neighboring towns, I would have access to over hundred properties. This is all within a ten-mile radius of my home. Why go farther?

2. Become an expert in an even smaller radius. It could be an area around your home, or it could be a neighboring town or a completely different area that you *believe* has excellent appreciation potential. This is a market that you will definitely find a few bargains in each year. For example, I recently spoke to a real estate investor who was becoming an expert in Cleveland, Ohio, though he lives in Manhattan.

3. Find sellers who are interested in selling quick. The reasons are varied:

   a. A couple may have just gotten divorced and the house is part of the settlement and neither wants to stay (or neither one can afford it)

   b. An illness occurred causing the owner(s) to move

   c. A job change requires the owner(s) to move and the company is paying for the transfer, thus, the owner may have less of an incentive to get top dollar for the sale

d. Money or real estate tax problems

e. Retiring owner(s) causing a move to a warmer or colder (yes, it does happen) climate

f. A real estate downturn in the area

So, how do you find these sellers? There are many ways. The most obvious is to go through local Realtors. You could put classified ads online on Craigslist or any of the real estate sites online, like the aforementioned Zillow.com or Realtor.com. You could run your own ads. You can just go and ring the bell of the houses that are for sale and talk to the owners. That will usually result in an even better outcome (but do your research first online).

Other ways to find owners who really want to sell, are by: (1) talking to friends in the area; (2) going to the banks (they may actually have properties that are foreclosures that they could work with you on); (3) going to the courthouses in the area you are targeting; (4) talking to accountants; and (5) finding real estate investment clubs in your area.

Now, how do you determine if the property is a good one? This scoring system is from *The One Minute Millionaire* by Mark Victor Hansen and Robert G. Allen. I love it for its simplicity, which is what this book is all about. They recommend rating the property by answering these five questions and scoring them with one point (poor), two points (average), or three points (excellent). Here are the five questions:

1. What is the price?

2. What is the property condition?

3. What are the terms—meaning, is the seller throwing in any extras? Do you have to do significant repairs? Can you move right in?

4. How is the location? Is it on a cul-de-sac or a busy, heavy-traffic street?

5. Is the seller highly motivated to sell?

Now, I would answer these questions yourself, but you might also want to ask the owner and the agent, if there is one, to also answer these questions.

If the property is at least an eleven, move forward with doing more due diligence. If not, I would recommend (as do Mark and Robert) moving on to the next property.

The additional due diligence you would then do would include many of the items that are standard in any home purchase. These would be: getting the property inspected by a home engineer to ensure there is no structural damage—minor or otherwise—who then recommends an exterminator to ensure there are no pests.

Once you've done your additional due diligence and no extra issues have come up, you should make an offer on those properties over 10!

I won't discuss the many ways you can buy property with no money down. I'd recommend that you purchase the best-selling book, *The One Minute Millionaire*, for Mark and Robert's detailed explanations. I will just say that, as already mentioned, you will use leverage to buy real estate. Even if you are putting 20, 30, or 40 percent down on a home, you can make a lot of money in real estate.

For example, you found a property that is a "12" and you have a motivated seller within the area that you consider your expertise. Suppose the house is going into foreclosure and you can scoop it up for $100,000 less than the average price of houses in the area, which happens to be $600,000. You buy the $500,000 property with a loan of $400,000 and cash of $100,000 (your own, or with a group of investors, or from your 'hard-money lender').

Suppose the monthly rental income on the property is $3,500, and as in the example above, your net operating income after expenses is $2,500 a month. The cap rate is 6 percent ($30,000 or $2,500 × 12 divided by $500,000). Not great! From an earnings perspective, it doesn't look like this is a great investment. But wait ...

That $100,000 in cash gives you access to a property that is likely worth $600,000. Now, let's assume you have to do some repairs that cost you $50,000. You make the repairs and put it back on the market six months later for $600,000, which is the price at which it sells.

Your $150,000 investment (the cash you put down—$100,000—plus the cost of repairs) appreciated $50,000 ($600,000 [the sale price]-$500,000 [the original cost of the property]-$50,000 [the cost of repairs] = $50,000). This is a 33 percent return ($50,000/$150,000) in just six months. That is, an annualized return of 66 percent, since you only held the property for one half of a year.

Now importantly, the above analysis assumes you did not rent out the property. It just assumes you made the repairs and put it back on the market for sale. But suppose all the repairs could be done while you had tenants. If that was the case, you could have achieved an additional return of $15,000 ($2,500 * 6) over the six months. Then, your return would have been an even more amazing 43.3 percent ($50,000 plus $15,000 divided by $150,000 or $65,000/$150,000) for six months. This is an annualized return of almost 87 percent!

That is the benefit of leverage!

Making a Smart Investment

Remember what I mentioned earlier: typically, low cap rate/high-dollar markets are purchased for value appreciation, and high cap rate/low-value markets are purchased for income. If you are buying for income in a low-value market, your potential for downward trending values may not affect you as much as markets where you buy for appreciation. Because you purchased for income, your rents should still cover your expenses. It is important to take note of the fact that buying expensive properties for price appreciation at the top of the market without the rent covering your expenses can be dangerous.

The most important aspect with any investment property is to ensure that the rental income will always cover your expenses (this includes covering the mortgage payment as well).

Here are three questions I have received from clients on real estate:

Isn't real estate just massive leverage?

What do you mean by "massive?" Real estate is absolutely a levered investment. You can put 10 or 20 percent down on a house or apartment building and get access to 100 percent of the capital. For example, say you find a great real estate investment in Michigan, outside of Detroit, for $150,000. If you were to invest $15,000 (you put 10 percent down), you would have access to the appreciation of the whole house—despite the fact that you have a mortgage on the house and the bank effectively owns it! So, if the house jumps 20 percent over the next year to $180,000, you will have earned 200 percent on your money (this is a simple example because it excludes closing costs involved in the sale of the property).

How?

Well, the appreciation was $30,000 and your investment was $15,000, and $30,000/15,000 is 200 percent, or two times.

Yes, there is leverage. I define leverage as the amount of investment you have access to divided by the amount you invested. In this example, the amount you have access to is $150,000 (when you invested) and the amount you put down is $15,000. Thus, your leverage is $150,000/$15,000 or 10 times. is this "massive"? It depends on your perspective.

Most margin stock accounts have two to three times leverage. That means if you put in $15,000 like we did in the real estate example, you would only be able to buy $30,000 to $45,000 of securities.

In the example, I gave in Part 2, Chapter 2: "Should I Use Credit?" the bank had leverage of 2 times. During the financial crisis in 2008, many banks had leverage of twenty times, and life insurance companies were levered fifteen times. This has dropped significantly, but life insurers still have asset leverage (assets divided by shareholders' equity) of eight to twelve times, and many banks have leverage of ten to fifteen times.

Why should I put my money in real estate? Don't you remember what happened in the collapse? It took years to get back to break-even!

Yes, it did! But, if you are a long-term investor, you still made money. I give people the example of houses in Westchester County, New York. Yes, they were clearly over-valued in 2006 and 2007 and into 2008 when they started declining. But if you bought with a ten-year or twenty-year time horizon, then even if you bought near the peak in 2007, as of 2017, you would be flat on your investment. And that is if you had the worst timing and only had a ten-year time horizon.

I generally recommend not investing in real estate unless you have a longer-term time horizon. And some diversification is better than none, unless of course, you have done all your due diligence and your upside to downside is significantly skewed to the upside.

This question is coming from a perspective of fear, lack, and worry. If you focus on the downside risk, you are more likely to lose money. I am not telling you to ignore it. Yes, be aware of it, but also be aware of the upside potential. Because of the leverage we just discussed, real estate—done right, with the proper analysis and planning—can make you very rich. And this is exactly because of the upside potential from leverage.

Am I looking in the right market?

Typically, high-dollar markets (i.e., Metro New York, San Francisco, Los Angeles in early 2019) do not provide good investments for income property (the rent may not cover your expenses because the values are too high), but these markets do provide good investments for price appreciation, if you can buy at the bottom of the market cycle. The problem is that if you buy for price appreciation at the top of the market cycle, you can find yourself in serious financial trouble. The best way to avoid this from happening is to buy in markets where all your expenses can be covered by the rental income from the property. The downside to this is the fact that typically, markets with good income potential may have values that trend downward or stay flat. The ideal situation is to buy in a market with solid income potential that has the potential for future value appreciation.

Key Points from Part 2, Chapter 6

- What is your belief level that you can use real estate to become rich? If it's at least an eight on a scale of one to ten, let's do this!
    - Remember, to be a great real estate investor, you have to be really good at just three things: (1) finding cheap properties; (2) finding cheap financing; and (3) selling the property at the right time.
- Use these simple suggestions for starting out in real estate:
    - Start with properties within a small distance from your house.
    - Become an expert in an even smaller radius.
    - Find sellers who are interested in selling quick.
- Answer these questions on a scale of one (poor) to three (excellent); two is average. Remember you are looking for structures that are at least an eleven to do more due diligence.
    - What is the price?
    - What is the property condition?
    - What are the terms? This means is the seller throwing in any extras? Do you have to do significant repairs? Is the house in move-in condition?
    - How is the location?
    - Is the seller highly motivated to sell?
- Leverage enhances your return at all times—unless you are putting 100 percent cash down. In our example, the investor earned a 33 percent return in just six months.

Conclusion

What are you now going to put in practice? I know whenever I finish a book, I don't take action on all the recommendations. A habit is sometimes difficult to establish, especially if you try doing too much all at once. So, I recommend starting with just one or two new items to add to your repertoire.

Which rule(s) resonated with you the most?

What do you *believe* and what do you *know* and have absolute faith in (Rule #1)?

Will you start writing down your level of belief in each investment idea you have from 1 (massive doubt) to 10 (absolute faith)?

Did you fill out your financial freedom survey to see all your beliefs about money? If not, you can go here: https://www.salaurmor.com/prosperity-survey/

Have you started trying to use your intuition (Rule #2) for everyday events—like picking which elevator to use in your office building or whether to take the highway or the local roads?

Have you even applied it to picking a security? How did it feel?

Have you started using some happy habits (Rule #3)? What are yours? Have you started journaling? How about meditating—for even five minutes a day? Are you doing random acts of kindness? What about exercising?

Have you start visualizing (Rule #4), even if it is for just three minutes a day? And are you experiencing the feeling of what it would be like to already have what you want? If yes, you will experience it even quicker.

Have you been thinking about what you are grateful for in your life (Rule #5)? Did you start a gratitude journal? Why not?

What about a giving program (Rule #6)? Do you have a favorite charity that you know will make a difference in the world? Start small—with just a few dollars—and build from there.

Have you started a budget (Rule #7)? Why not? Just track all your expenses for one day. You can do that!

What investments resonate with you? Can you do it yourself (Rule #8)? Are they stocks or bonds or real estate?

What are you passionate about that you know you can take responsibility for and have fun with too?

Now find the best ideas in that asset class. Not a hundred, not twenty—just a few! What is the right number for you? And don't diversify (Rule #9)!

Why not pick one or two rules and do them for twenty-one days. Think about which one or two items resonate with you.

You can do this! Start small. Don't get overwhelmed. By using just one or two items, you have begun your journey to financial freedom. But here is another way:

Please go online to https://www.salaurmor.com/. Sign up for your 30 minutes of free prosperity coaching!

If you enjoyed this book and think it was worth at least what you paid for it, then please tell your friends and family. I do want to help as many people as possible become financially free. You would be doing them a great service if you mentioned the book to them.

Finally, thanks for reading! I believe in you!

If you love the book (or even liked it) and have a moment to spare, I would really appreciate a short review, as this helps new readers find my books.

Appendix

Powerful Affirmations

"Say them *every* day!"

"Literally? You want me to say them every single day?"

"Yes!"

"You really think Napoleon Hill meant that?"

"Yes. I do."

This is a conversation I had with one of my clients in 2018 after I suggested he read the "Self-Confidence" affirmation that Hill has in his international best seller, *Think and Grow Rich*.

As I explained in *Mindful Money Management*, affirmations are carefully constructed statements, said out loud or silently, which can transform your thoughts and ultimately your future. I find them more powerful when stated out loud. They are very useful, repetitive statements that should be charged with emotion. In short, items are more likely to manifest into your life quicker when repetition is used in conjunction with emotion, and not as a stand-alone strategy.

Affirmations are really powerful, and if you do them regularly, they *will* change your life.

Again, start small. Pick just one or two. This is how I started in the early 2000s. It required only a minute or two.

Now, as of this book's writing in 2018, I spend fifteen to twenty minutes reading my affirmations.

Here is the affirmation from Mr. Hill that I had recommended to my client:

"I know I have the ability to achieve the object of my definite purpose in life, therefore, I demand of myself persistent, continuous action towards its attainment, and I here and now promise to render such action.

"I realize the dominating thoughts of my mind will eventually reproduce themselves in outward, physical action and gradually transform themselves into physical reality, therefore I will concentrate my thoughts for thirty minutes daily upon the task of thinking of the person I intend to become, thereby creating in my mind a clear mental picture of that person.

"I will devote ten minutes per day to demanding of myself the development of self-confidence.

"I have clearly written down a description of my chief aim in life and I will never stop trying until I have developed sufficient self-confidence for its attainment.

"I fully realize that no wealth or position can endure unless built upon truth and justice and therefore, I will engage in no transaction which does not benefit all whom it affects. I will succeed by attracting to myself the forces I wish to use and the cooperation of other people.

"I will induce others to serve me because of my willingness to serve others. I will eliminate hatred, envy, jealousy, selfishness, and cynicism by developing love for all humanity because I know that a negative attitude towards others can never bring me success. I will cause others to believe in me because I believe in them and myself."

Of course, the next questions were: (1) do I really have to concentrate for thirty minutes daily, and (2) do I really have to do ten minutes of self-confidence work every day?

My answer is: if you want to become the person in your mind and if you do indeed want to improve your self-esteem, then yes, take forty minutes out of every day to do that. I'm sure you can find forty minutes from all the little bits of wasted time we discussed earlier.

But again, you can build up to this amount of time over many months (or even years).

I can tell you personally that I waste at least thirty minutes almost every day playing Ruzzle, and checking Instagram and Facebook on my phone. Eliminating these wasted moments can indeed change your life.

I recommend another powerful affirmation every morning from *Think and Grow Rich* if you don't yet know your chief aim in life or you have a sense of it, but have not made it a specific goal yet:

"Before 'x date', I will have in my possession 'y dollars' of net worth which will come to me in various amounts from time to time in the interim.

"In return for this money, I will give the most efficient service of which I am capable, rendering the fullest possible quantity and the best possible quality of service.

"I believe I will have this money in my possession. My faith is so strong that I can now see this money before my eyes. I can touch it with my hands. It is now awaiting transfer to me in the proportion that I deliver the service I intend to render for it. I am awaiting a plan by which to accumulate this money and I will follow this plan when it is received.

"I will give at least at 10 percent to various charities including (decide on a specific charitable contribution to give to and put it in your affirmation)."

Though I tell my clients not to set deadlines for their goals since it will only create stress and worry as you approach the "due date," I think if "x date" is far enough in the future, that it does not stress or worry you and you still would be ecstatic if you achieved this amount of money by that date, then put a date on your goal.

I found the two following affirmations from *The One Minute Millionaire* particularly powerful. I'd highly recommend reading these daily as well.

"Today I am enough.

I am smart enough.

Wise enough.

Clever enough.

Resourceful enough

Able enough.

Confident enough.

I am connected to enough people to accomplish my heart's desire.

I have enough ideas to pull off magic and miracles.

Enough is all I need.

Enough is what I have.

I have more than enough.

As I do all that I can do, I'm able to do more and more. I am excited to be alive … I am passionately on-purpose to do good, be good, and help others do the same. I am enough. I have enough. I do enough."

"In this life, there are givers and takers. I am a giver. I like to give. I love to give. Giving is my way of life. I give away my ideas to great causes that I care deeply about. I give money where it is needed, is wanted, and can do enormous amounts of good. My giving always creates more. I inspire others to give and like doing it. It is my subtle mission to give and motivate other rich people to give … Giving is one of the main reasons that I enjoy being a millionaire. I make millions. I save millions. I invest millions. I give millions away."

This affirmation from *The Magic of Thinking Big* can be found here https://www.salaurmor.com/manifesting/, but I wanted to include it in the book as well because I highly recommend saying it daily:

"(YOUR NAME), meet (YOUR NAME): an important, really important person. (YOUR NAME) is a big thinker, so think big. Think big about everything. You've got plenty of ability to do a first-class job. So, do a first-class job. (YOUR NAME), you believe in happiness, progress, and prosperity. So talk only happiness, progress, and prosperity. You have lots of drive (YOUR NAME), lots of drive. So, put that drive to work. Nothing can stop you, (YOUR NAME), nothing. You are enthusiastic! Let your enthusiasm show. You look good, (YOUR NAME), and you feel good. Stay that way. (YOUR NAME), you were a great gal (guy) yesterday; you're going to be an even greater gal (guy) today. Now go to it, (YOUR NAME). Go forward!!"

I have a favorite affirmation from Sandy Forster's best seller, *Wildly Wealthy Fast*, called the Abundance Affirmation which I alluded to in Part 2, Chapter 1.

Here it is:

"I am unlimited. I now consciously and subconsciously flood every atom of my body, mind and spirit with Prosperity Consciousness. I bless everyone in the Universe to have Abundance and Prosperity.

I give myself permission to deserve and expect Abundance and Prosperity. I call Abundance and Prosperity from the four corners of the earth and throughout the Universe.

Prosperity in the north, south, east and west – come to me now!

Abundance in the north, south, east and west – come to me now!

187

Money in the north, south, east and west – come to me now!

Riches in the north, south, east and west – come to me now!

Wealth in the north, south, east and west – come to me now!

And so it is – and I love it!"

In Hal Elrod's eye-opening book, *The Miracle Morning*, he shares a few of his affirmations. Try saying this one every morning and see how you feel:

"There is nothing to fear because you can't fail. Only learn, grow and become better than you have ever been before. I have arrived at this moment to learn what I must learn so that I can become the person I need to be to create everything I've ever wanted for my life. Even when life is difficult or challenging—especially when life is difficult and challenging—the present is an opportunity for us to learn, grow, and become better than we've ever been before!"

I must conclude this Appendix on affirmations with a very powerful one from Mike and Andy Dooley. They recommend saying it out loud. Say it daily!

"I now know my divinity!

I am clear and confident.

I am a leader.

I am guided by love.

I am vibrating infinite possibilities!

I celebrate the contrast.

I rock!

I love my life!

I am the creator!"

Key Points from Appendix:

- Pick at least two affirmations and say them as part of your daily morning routine.

- Email me on https://www.salaurmor.com/ if you would like to know the affirmations I am currently doing for prosperity, abundance, and to manifest your dreams and desires quicker.

About the Author

Joel Salomon is a prosperity coach who helps others overcome obstacles standing in the way of their financial freedom. In 2018, he published *Mindful Money Management: Memoirs of a Hedge Fund Manager*, which immediately became a Best Seller.

Joel is also an award-winning speaker and frequent podcast guest. He has led 9 workshops teaching the concepts of how to overcome limiting beliefs. He has spoken at numerous Rotary and Lions' Clubs in the New York Metropolitan area and at Mercy College's MBA program, as well as at Mike Dooley's Infinite Possibilities Training Conference in New Orleans in March 2018.

He appeared on TV with CEO Money and has also been a guest on more than 20 podcasts including *Every Day is a New Day Show*, the Award-Winning *Nice Guys* Podcast, *The Financial Survival Network*, and *Think, Believe, Manifest*. Joel has also been quoted in the Wall Street Journal, Newsday, U.S. News and World Report, and interviewed in Forbes and on Bloomberg Radio.

In 2012, he achieved a decades-long dream with the launch of his own hedge fund, SaLaurMor Capital (named after his two daughters, Lauren and Morgan).

Salomon's financial experience includes managing long/short equity and credit portfolios for Citi, with an emphasis on asset managers, insurers, and specialty financial companies. Salomon generated positive returns every year during his time at Citi, including 2008, when the market suffered 40 percent losses.

Salomon has been a Chartered Financial Analyst since 1995. In 1992, he was named a Fellow of the Society of Actuaries. He is also an Advanced Communicator Gold Toastmaster and a Certified Infinite Possibilities Trainer & Trailblazer.

When not helping others achieve their financial dreams, Salomon enjoys table tennis, bowling, and skiing. He is also an avid traveler and has visited over forty countries and five continents.